I See You

Nancy Nystrom

Founder
Casa Hogar Los Angelitos

Nancy and Little Lupita—We see
through loving eyes.

I See You

©2021 by Nancy Nystrom

ISBN 978-0-692-62283-4

Published by
The Children's Foundation
tcfcares.org

The Children's Foundation
P. O. Box 688
Fulshear, Texas 77441
Printed in the United States of America

Editing and layout by Martha W. Nichols, aMuse Productions,
Fort Collins, Colorado, USA

Introduction	1
Foreword	8
Author's Prelude	9
Author's Disclaimer	10
Heroes	14
Driving Change	19
The Garbage Dump	23
Ricardo	25
The Slagg Family	30
Brenda and the Indy 500	38
I See You!	48
I Knew You Even Before You Were Born	62
Unconditional Love	75
Daniel	78
Discipline/Consequences	82
The Cartels	86
Pilar	97
Emigdia	100
Their Mouths Will Be Full! (They Will Have To Eat Their Words!)	107
Transforming Lives	118
The Continuation	139
Putting It Together	143
Appendix	160
References	162
But the Greatest Gift Is Love!	168

This book is dedicated to all those who have been part of Casa Hogar Los Angelitos during these past twenty-two-plus years, to all those who are yet to come, to the beautiful children of Mexico, and especially to my husband Dave—the hero of my life.

Dave with first group of children at CHLA.

Introduction

Tackling a second book or sequel can be a daunting task. In *I See You*, Nancy Nystrom again speaks to us in her unique voice and gives her readers a deeper insight into the lives that have been dramatically touched by her life's work, Casa Hogar Los Angelitos. Nancy's beautiful gift of really seeing the people God has placed in her path is an inspiration for us to pause and take a visual inventory of the precious people in our lives. As this book and the stories within began to develop it was clear that Nancy and the children she has empowered have more to tell us and more to teach us.

For me, these special stories have become personal as my life has been interwoven with many of them. The privilege of a front row seat for several years has made some things clear to me. There is no way around the fact that education gives opportunity to anyone lucky enough to grasp it. As Malala Yousafzai says, "One child, one teacher, one book, one pen can change the world." Casa Hogar Los Angelitos has seen the evidence of this in the faces of so many of the children. When they begin to learn to read, catch up to their grade level, graduate from one level to the next, they feel invincible. They feel like they can do anything; they feel like they can change the world!

In 2018, Casa Hogar had three former residents graduate from high school. Julio, Juan, and Meredith are forever changed because of the opportunity they have had to reach this milestone. The door to the future has been opened for them and we are celebrating! In addition; Laura, Ricky, and Anabel are all pursuing college degrees. We also celebrated Artemio's graduation from the University of Colima in 2018. What a great success! There are now three college graduates who grew up in the casa hogar! Many incredible kids are coming up behind these and looking with hope towards their own futures.

Another thing that is clear to me is that education is multi-dimensional. It is important that children do not just have their minds educated but are given opportunities for their hearts and spiritual identities to grow as well. In a balanced and whole approach, Casa Hogar is focused not only on the life changing benefits of education but on each child's health and psychological wellness. Aristotle is credited with saying, "Educating the mind without educating the heart is no education at all." The multidimensional healing happening at Casa Hogar includes being cared for along with learning values and positive character traits. Additionally, it is important for each child to understand that they were created by God and he loves them unconditionally and without exception. That He has seen them and has an important plan for their life. The goal is not only for the kids to have a bright future but for them to be a shining light into the

Our first three college graduates.

future, making the world a better place because of who they are.

Just like you and me, all they needed was for someone to come alongside them and say, "I see you, and I believe you can do it."

Enjoy these amazing stories, and let this book be the catalyst for you in your life to look people in the eye and tell them, "You are worth my time, my energy, and my love—just because you are you."

—*Melanie D. Kolb, BA Family Psychology*

The first time I walked through the doors of Casa Hogar Los Angelitos, I knew something truly special was happening in Manzanillo.

My family and I arrived in the city on one of our annual visits and I had finally asked a neighbor at our condo if I could visit "the orphanage." I had come to know many American and Canadian snowbirds who spoke at great length about the success of Casa Hogar Los Angelitos, and the unique model of holistic care they had developed for children.

Visiting an orphanage is not something one would typically plan during a family vacation to Mexico, however, the influence that this orphanage made on me has been felt for longer than any tourist activity I can recollect.

There is an extraordinary sense of warmth and love that seems to resonate within the orphanage, as if the walls themselves have been seasoned by years of music, dancing and laughter. Aside from receiving regular meals and a warm bed to sleep in, children at Casa Hogar Los Angelitos participate in daily art and education programs, created and developed over years by Nancy and her dedicated team.

These programs teach children new skills while helping them buyild the confidence they need to overcome emotional traumas caused by years of abuse and neglect. The focus on expressive arts is just a part of the essential building blocks that have helped the children of Casa Hogar Los Angelitos go on to have such great success in life.

After speaking with Nancy and learning the story of how Casa Hogar Los Angelitos came to be, I decided that the world must know about this wonderful place. I believe that if others could learn about this organization, they could replicate its practices and expand this model to other parts of the world.

I brought the story of Casa Hogar Los Angelitos back to my company in Canada and pitched the idea to make a film about Nancy and the orphanage in 2019, we began filming "*Unconditional*," a story of the triumph at Casa Hogar Los Angelitos in Manzanillo, Mexico.

I am honored to share my thoughts as a foreword to Nancy's new book, which gives readers even greater insight into the challenges that vulnerable children are facing throughout Mexico, and shows the opportunities gained when they walk through the doors of Casa Hogar Los Angelitos.

—*Kevin Haluk*
Managing Director
SmartCast Goup
Vancouver, Canada

I started visiting Casa Hogar Los Angelitos almost 20 years ago. When I discovered what Nancy and Dave were doing in the lives of the children of Casa Hogar Los Angelitos, I wanted to introduce kids in the United States to this children's home. I knew that if kids in the U.S. could see what was happening at this amazing place, it would have a profound effect on their lives. As a result, I have been bringing groups of student athletes on service learning trips to Casa Hogar for almost 10 years. The effect that Nancy and the children of the casa hogar have had on these girls from the U.S has been life changing, and I have the stories to prove it! There is something special about this story that affects people in the most profound way, and I believe it's simply the power of love combined with amazingly intuitive programs to promote healing.

It was during my second trip to the casa hogar that we were attempting to deliver supplies to the poor village of La Lima when suddenly the vehicle that Nancy and I were riding in had *two* flat tires *at the same time*! Needless to say, we spent several hours stuck in a dried-up riverbed waiting for help! It was during this unfortunate circumstance that I got to hear about Nancy's vision for Casa Hogar firsthand. To hear Nancy tell the stories included in her first book, *Each Day a Portion*, changed my life forever. It was at that time that I dedicated a large portion my life to supporting this project and exposing girls in the U.S. to the principals of love that flow from the excellent environment of the casa hogar.

I'm very excited that Nancy wrote *I See You* as a follow up to *Each Day a Portion* because it provides the proof that her and Dave's calling changed the lives of thousands of people in the U.S., Canada and Mexico. To hear all that Nancy and CHLA has had to overcome in order to save children from the streets of Manzanillo is an amazing story in and of itself. But to hear in *I See You*, how the love flowing from Casa Hogar has played out in the lives of some of the first children, is a profound story of human achievement. It has been one of the most rewarding experiences of my life to be a witness to the transforming effect of Casa Hogar Los Angelitos. I will continue to bring groups down to Manzanillo as this is the most life transforming experiences anyone could ever have.

I am so thankful to have met Dave and Nancy Nystrom. They have followed a vision from above and now have impacted thousands of lives. Their commitment to these children and the love they have provided is what we are all sent here to do which is to love and help all those that we come into contact with. Dave and Nancy, thank you for having the guts to see this vision through and I hope you realize how many lives you have changed. Your amazing legacy will be one to be admired. Thanks for letting me be a part of your vision...and we are not done yet! Love never fails!

—Kevin Skeens

Owner and Master Coach
Ballistic Volleyball Club, Broomfield, Colorado
Founder of Try Love, former Director of Development of
The Children's Foundation
Bachelor of Arts in Social Science
Certified Mental Toughness Coach
International Mental Game Coaches Association

Foreword

> With every ounce of breath they could muster, they stood on the side of the road and screamed. The crowds silenced the blind beggars, scolding them to be quiet. Yet they would not be gagged; they continued crying out to Jesus, "Have mercy on us!" Their lives depended on being seen. Jesus saw them, had compassion for them and gave them sight.
>
> —*Matthew 20:29-34*

Healing begins only by being seen. Whether graced or learned (more likely both), Nancy Nystrom has the gift of seeing. She sees the little broken boy, abandoned by his father, abused by a priest. She sees the wary and worn face of a nine year old girl from the dump who is the caregiver for her tiny siblings. Nancy has a gift to see and to help us see.

We avert our eyes from the blind men, the broken boys, the abandoned girls. We want to silence them from clamoring in our world. Yet the call of Jesus is for us to stop and see. To hear their stories and have compassion.

Nancy has heard and not silenced. Nancy has heard, taken in, embraced, and unleashed healing for countless boy and girls, young men and women. By seeing them, Nancy has enabled them to see.

In the following pages, Nancy Nystrom invites us to join her in this healing journey of seeing. A wise guide, she will teach us how to see. I am thankful for Nancy as she has helped our church, LifeSpring Covenant Church, stop for those we might have otherwise ignored. We are forever indebted to Nancy for inviting us to be partners in seeing the children at Casa Hogar Los Angelitos. In the seeing, not only are they healed, but so are we.

Pastor Scott Slayback
LifeSpring Covenant Church
Loveland, Colorado

Author's Prelude

This is not intended to be a religious book, but it would be impossible to write about this work without including faith, because it was through faith that I found the strength and determination to keep going when the odds were against me and the long-term success of the project. It was faith that enabled me to look beyond the criticisms, the failures, the frustrations, threats, and abandonment by others in order to continue, and faith that kept me believing. A good friend of mine said to me one day "Nancy, you seem to have so much faith, I wish I had your faith." I have to honestly say that sometimes my faith is weak, and many times I struggled with faith during difficult times, and faith didn't come automatically to me. It became a choice…every day I chose to believe; I chose faith.

This book is not about only the children of Mexico, but also it is about humanity, and how similar life struggles can be, regardless of where you live. It also touches on our responsibility to recognize disparities, to make a conscience effort to cause change, advance children's rights, and to look beyond the skin color, economic situation, and outward appearance in order to really see those who are suffering. That can feel really scary and seem like a lot to think about, but nothing ever changes if we don't take responsibility to change the way we view things.

Author's Disclaimer

I am not a psychologist, so I have no credentials to stand on other than being a mother, my other life experiences, years of observations working with children, and my determination to positively change the lives of children.

People have encouraged me to write a second book telling more stories of the children that have called Casa Hogar Los Angelitos home. As I move forward to write a continuation of the first book *Each Day a Portion* I am nervous, faced with the dilemma of how to keep people's attention so they will actually read and finish this second book. I spend hours polishing a sentence, choosing the right word, hoping to make a laborious effort appear effortless and natural, and yet I am unsure of whether it is even worthy of reading. I will leave that determination to each of you as you wander through these true stories.

Writing about the excitement and struggles of beginning a work like Casa Hogar Los Angelitos seems a lot more interesting than writing about the continuation and the day-to-day challenges, heartbreaks, and successes.

My friend Don Miller, an inspirational speaker and international sales trainer, often uses a historical quote supposedly from Genghis Khan.

Genghis Khan, one of history's most successful conquerors, knew what he was talking about when he said

> It's easy to conquer the world on horseback—
> not so easy to dismount and govern.

Genghis Khan put fear into hearts everywhere he went. I hope I don't do that, , but I can definitely relate to the "not so easy to govern" part.

Names of the children have been changed in order to protect their privacy and respect their dignity. The only exceptions are those who are now adults and who have chosen to write their own stories and use their own names. Some of the children who were included in the book *Each Day a Portion* are now adults. Their stories have continued, and I will include some of them when appropriate.

I am flying in to Manzanillo from Mexico City. My heart starts to flutter, and I find myself getting excited as I see the familiar terrain. I look across the sky to see if the volcano is visible, but seldom does our flight come in from the east close enough to see that magnificent fire breathing mountain. How can a place, another world, evoke

Colima Volcano del Fuego during active period

so many emotions? Another world…yet so much *my* world.

All the memories. The last time I saw Fred, the first time I met Lupita, Dr. Guiber, the trips down the coast with Rob and Felipe to the best surfing beaches. My stepfather Paul and the special funeral the Pelayo girls had for him. Paul had said., "What better place to die than on the beach of Manzanillo?"

I laugh as I think about the flights we used to take on the now-defunct AeroCalifornia, always the same pink bathroom and duct tape holding the panel erect.

Miles and miles of regal coconut palms greet us as we fly in, hiding the banana trees with their blue plastic bags hanging off each stalk, the perfectly prepared fields of chilies and tomatoes, and then there is that same stretch of abandoned pavement leading from the airport, destroyed and broken down by one of the hurricanes a few years ago. It probably will remain unrepaired or replaced for who knows how many more years… just there as a reminder of what might have been.

I am anxious to see everyone. Anxious to see the familiar fields of papaya, lime, and mango trees and to hear the sound of the waves slapping against the beach.

Ah, Manzanillo.

I am home.

Heroes

At 10 P.M., Benjamin noticed a red pickup parked behind the casa hogar with two men, lights off, facing the entrance to the drug and alcohol rehab center, watching the activities on the street. He held his sixteen-ounce cola bottle tighter and continued on to his home, Casa 3.

At 3 A.M., *Pop!pop!...pop pop pop...!* like a display of fireworks on the other side of the wall. A series of gunshots, yelling, sharp blasts of police sirens, and sounds of people running down the street pierced the calm of the night.

The older girls on the top floor could hear the echoes so loud it was as if the shots and voices were in their room. All they could do was cover their heads, crouch together in huddles, shaking in fear as they listened to a barrage of bullets coming from the street behind the casa hogar. The screeching of the sirens was almost as stressful as the gunfire. A police officer was shot, and one of the *ladrones* (criminals) jumped over the wall of the rehab center trying to escape. More shots… then the squealing of tires as the truck sped away and it was all over, at least on our street.

By 6 A.M., all was quiet.

The girls showered, dressed, and prepared to leave for school as if nothing had happened.

As a young girl, I liked to pretend to be one of the many heroes I read about or watched on our black-and-white TV: Roy Rogers or Hopalong Cassidy (it's always good if you can have an action name like *Hopalong*) with his horse Topper, or the Lone Ranger with his partner Tonto and his familiar "Hi yo Silver! Awaaaaay!!" call to action as he dramatically rears his horse, charging after the bad guys or going to someone's rescue. However, my favorite was Robin Hood, because I could make his pointed hat out of a brown paper bag. That gave me a prop and authenticity.

Even though, as I look back, I realize that most of my heroes were men, I never considered that in my decision nor did I call myself Robina Hood. I could have been Lady Marian, but I preferred to be a "real" hero like Roy Rogers or Robin Hood. Saving the day!

Wonder Woman came a little later, and of course I could never have been Wonder Woman with her bathing suit hero outfit. I wasn't even allowed to wear *shorts* when I was growing up, much less run around in a bathing suit!

Today, after traveling to my great, great, great-grandfather Hogan's beautiful Ireland so many times and loving the romanticism and legends of that spirited people, I think I would like to be—or at least be related to—"Galloping Hogan," a folk hero during the fight for Irish independence in the late 1600s. I really like his name!

The Irish, who seem to have so much in common with the Mexicans, were always fighting for or against something—uprisings, oppression, religion, and so on—but this battle was especially important and bravely fought, although eventually lost.

Some historians believe Galloping Hogan was one of several thousand heroes who later became referred to as the "Wild Geese," revolutionary leaders and Irish lords who were permanently exiled from their beloved Ireland for their role in this battle for independence. "Galloping Hogan" was a fearless *rapparee* or highwayman (see page 163). Legend has him as the Robin Hood of Ireland. Even his "action" name makes him a hero for me.

We read about the heroes of the Bible, the heroes of history, the heroes of today who come from all walks of life and champion so many different worthy causes....

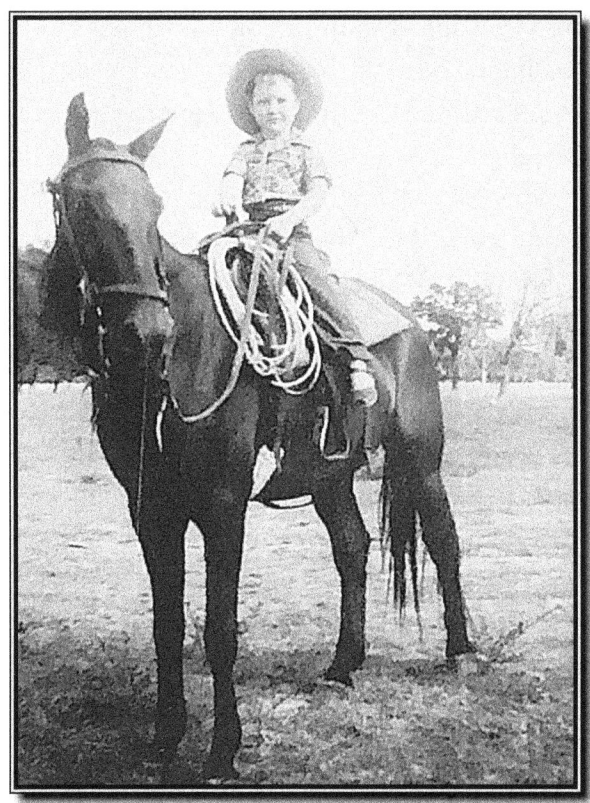

Nancy: Galloping Hogan? Or was it Hopalong Cassidy? Most children like to pretend and act out characters or heroes they may have read about, seen, or can imagine.

However, today, the heroes in my life are the children I have seen who overcome extreme abuse, abandonment, neglect, fear, and other heart-breaking circumstances and with sheer determination have turned their lives around from despair to success.

Most children like to pretend and act out characters or heroes they have read about, seen, or can imagine. Brianna accompanied her mother traveling with cross-country truckers; by an early age, she learned to flirt with the men as if part of a game.

When she entered the casa hogar, she had already learned to pretend she was a table dancer like her mother. Like most children, Brianna's mother was her hero—she was all Brianna had known and seen. As a child, her dream was to be like her mother.

I pretended to be Robin Hood—Brianna pretended to be a table dancer. Brianna entered the casa hogar with her older brother at the age of 6. After a little more than two years in the casa hogar Brianna's mother came and asked permission to take her for an ice cream...but she never came back. Brianna didn't have the chance to find new heroes or to see the potential of her life outside of truckers, abusive men, and quasi-prostitution.

Driving Change

Probably because of my Irish heritage, the centuries of Irish oppression and poverty is a subject close to my heart. One of my favorite books was Frank McCourt's *Angela's Ashes*, a poignant biography of suffering, growing up in the extreme poverty of Ireland during the early 1900s:

> When I look back on my childhood I wonder how I survived at all. It was, of course, a miserable childhood: the happy childhood is hardly worth your while. Worse than the ordinary miserable childhood is the miserable Irish childhood, and worse yet is the miserable Irish Catholic childhood.
>
> *Frank McCourt* Angela's Ashes

The plight of his family and so many other Irish families continues to touch me as I think about the situations and hardships that people, especially women and children, must have gone through during those difficult times.

Some of the most haunting Irish songs were written during the famine years and the decades after. *Athenry*, *Carrickfergus*, and so many more; all lamenting terrible struggles; the home they had to leave, the lost love, hopes and dreams, all left behind in desperation as they struggled to find new hope in a new life, immigrating to new worlds.

We happened to be in Limerick during the filming of McCourt's book and watched some of the scenes coming together from the tower of King John's Castle. As we walked back over the bridge crossing the Limerick river an animated older woman came scurrying across, mumbling and shaking her head. Then as we passed each other she blurted out, "terrible!, terrible! It's a disgrace!" I smiled and nodded to her, and she grumpily pointed to where they were filming and said, "That book! It's terrible! Terrible!" Apparently, she didn't approve of the negative light it cast on Limerick, the church, or the Irish people. This lady (who might well have been alive during the time in question) did not want to believe that situations like the McCourt family really existed. She was likely embarrassed, or maybe she just didn't approve of dirty laundry being aired in public.

A young Mexican man that I was working with several years ago would get upset with me every time I gave statistics about poverty, prostitution, child trafficking, or any of the other severe situations that I thought needed to be addressed. He was offended that I might put Mexico (which I dearly love) in a bad light. Finally, I said to him, "The biggest problem that Mexico and other countries have is the refusal of people with resources to realize that a problem exists! A situation has to be acknowledged first in order to cause change."

Perhaps the devastation and abuse could have been prevented, or at the very least been relieved, if those in power, control and capacity to cause change, had acknowledged what was happening and had chosen to do something during the great Irish famine. Where were the heroes? It is difficult to change a situation if, according to common belief, it doesn't exist.

Recently, I read an article published by UNICEF that talks about this attitude and this issue.

"UNICEF has learned through experience that problems that go unmeasured often go unsolved.

> We believe that consistent, credible data about children's situations are critical to the improvement of their lives—and indispensable to realizing the rights of every child. Data continues to support advocacy and action

on behalf of the world's 2.2 billion children, providing governments with facts on which to base decisions and actions to improve children's lives.Data does not, of itself, change the world. It makes change possible; by identifying needs, supporting advocacy, and gauging progress."
—*(quote from UNICEF article)*

Throughout the Western Hemisphere there are the difficult issues of determining and monitoring the care of children, whether in the family home, foster care, children's homes, or other programs. This might be the most important issue that we deal with.

We didn't have the authority to take Brianna away from her mother, or to "re-rescue" her. So she was lost to her "fate" in life. I have kept in touch with her over the years and have seen the pain-filled life that she has accepted simply because she didn't have the opportunity to choose the right heroes.

A few years ago, Brianna's young daughter came to us through social services asking for help. She had the courage to ask her mother to bring her to the casa hogar so she could go to school. I hoped that perhaps this time there would be an opportunity to break that cycle of perceived fate—to give Brianna's daughter different heroes. That hope was shattered when the grandmother, Brianna's mother, came and took Brianna out of the casa hogar—a sad repeat of history.

The Garbage Dump

As we look at difficult situations in the world there is one story that repeats itself too many times

Imagine you are a nine-year-old girl living under a plastic cover in the town's garbage dump, rummaging for food in the trash and fighting the heat and odors of such a filthy place. Imagine looking for food for yourself and your six younger siblings among the rats and hungry animals...alone, crying, hungry, and frightened. Can you imagine not knowing your last name, your birthday, or that you even exist in the eyes of society? That is the reality for many children throughout the world and the reality for a family brought in to the casa hogar a few years ago.

The two youngest children of this family were taken by the social service agencies and (we assume) adopted out. The other five were brought to us. I remember the day these five arrived, dirty, confused, full of *amebas* and infestations. The social service agency brought them in without paperwork other than permission for us to care for them. They didn't have information regarding their family, their last names, birthdates, or ages. The children only knew their first names. We had to immediately begin the process to 'de-infest' them and to prevent contamination of the other children.

It took several years to complete the legal work, birth certificates, and birthdays, and for them to be given an official last name.

I think about how they have blossomed during these years. They are smart and they work hard to be successful. They are talented and charming. What if they had never been given a chance? What if they had been left to their "fate"? What if no one ever noticed? What if no one could see them?

They are no longer "children from the dump." Today, they are beautiful, healthy, and successful. Life now has opportunity and hope. This September, one of those children entered the university to begin studying for her career.

Whereas not all children come from a garbage dump, sometimes it can be just as sad.

Ricardo

Ricardo came to us from another facility when he was 11 years old. We had been contacted by this facility to take Ricardo. He was now going into puberty and had what they referred to as a "trouble-making" attitude.

From the beginning I knew he was special. He kept asking about angels. Are they real, what do they look like, how do I know? He was very sensitive and extremely shy. He participated in art classes at the casa hogar, began to draw, and we soon discovered that he had an amazing natural talent!

The first time I really had the opportunity to talk with him was at our house during a group swimming party. I noticed that he wouldn't go into the pool with the other kids so I asked him to come sit with me and talk. Asking him why he didn't go into the pool he shyly answered, "because I don't want to take off my *playera* (t-shirt)." I asked, "Why is that, Ricardo?" He kind of shrugged his shoulders and said, "I am too fat and white."

Being a chubby, extremely white girl who never wanted to expose my whiteness in a swim suit, I totally got it. "Well, Ricardo, you don't have to take off your *playera*...just go in and have fun. However, I want to know if you know how to swim."

Although Manzanillo is on the ocean, most of the population never learns to swim. Ricardo grinned and said, "Yes, I learned at the other casa hogar." Oh, OK…. I asked, "Ricardo, why did you leave the other casa hogar?"

He casually said, "They didn't want me anymore." I couldn't stop myself from putting my arms around him and saying, "Ricardo, this is now your home. I'm glad you are here…I want you here. I will never ask you to leave!" He smiled, said, "Gracias," and then turned and went running to the pool. I've had to remember those words a few times during his teen years when he continued to struggle with his attitude…but I'm glad I didn't go back on my word. Ricardo is now at the university studying architecture and he has written some of his story for me to share with you.

Ricardo

My name is Ricardo. My mother abandoned me when I was very little, leaving me with my father, who was already old at 65. (Well, nobody really knows for sure how old he is because my grandparents never legally registered him.)

My father intended to put my sisters and me in an orphanage. He took my sisters to Manzanillo and me to Queretaro. My experience in Queretaro was horrible. The orphanage was run by a Catholic priest, who really didn't take care of the children. The place where he lived was an abandoned house, without lights, and smelled bad from dampness. It had one bed at the back where there was a lot of concrete debris. The bed smelled like urine. I hated that place.

I ran away from that orphanage, and before I left the priest told me that I would regret leaving, but I told him I would NEVER return. I don't remember how old I was, but I must have been seven or eight years old. I went to live on the street. One day I was close to a ditch where I think I almost got eaten by a crocodile, but someone came and saved me. I don't really remember how that happened; I just remember I was very frightened. Then this family found me and took me to live with them. Several months passed and my old father came to look for me. But I didn't care because I had stopped loving my father. I felt he had abandoned me too.

When my father couldn't find me at the orphanage, he went to the police to report me kidnapped. They found me living with this other family that I liked, but they took me away and returned me to my father.

When I lived with my father, he would hit me sometimes so hard that I had big bruises on my legs for weeks. Finally, the teachers at school talked with my father and he stopped hitting me so hard.

I was almost eleven years old when my father took me to the same orphanage where my sisters were in Manzanillo. The nuns who were in charge of that place made an arrangement with my father for him to pay them to take care of me. But when my father couldn't pay anymore, they told him that I couldn't live there anymore. My father took me back with him to the farm for a couple of months, and then he took me to Casa Hogar Los

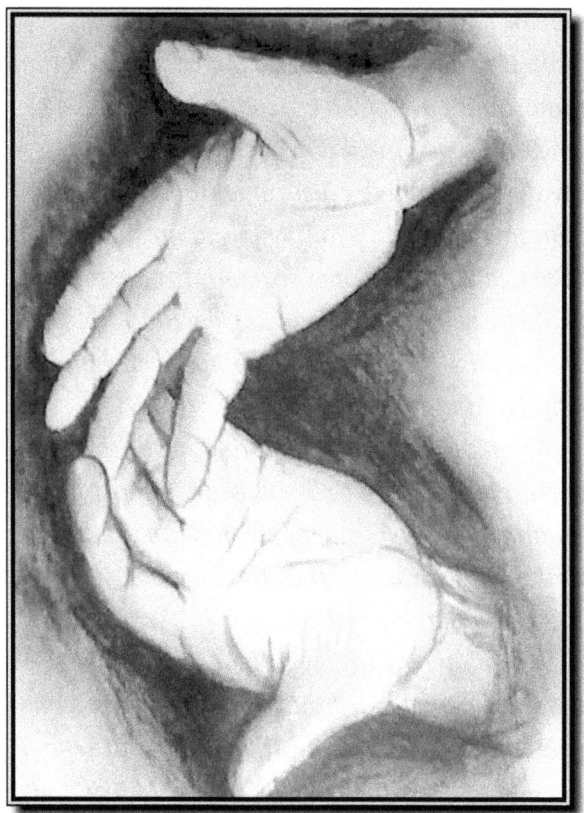

Ricardo's self-portrait: "Because I have only my hands and mind to change my future...with strength, intelligence, love, and talent."

Angelitos, where I have now grown up and will continue my education at the University to be an architect.

I have had the opportunity to talk to my mother and to know more about her, things I didn't know before, but things that helped me to understand why she did what she did. My mother was abandoned and grew up in an orphanage like me, and when she married my father, she was only 20 and he was 60 years old. I think she had a very hard time.

It is interesting that the family of my father (all his older children) tell my sisters and me that he is not our real father. This hurts me, but I don't

He will redeem them from oppression and violence, for their lives are precious to Him.

know the truth. I feel that my life has been very sad, but I have dreams for the future. I am hoping that my life can be happy, that I can overcome my past, and someday be successful. I would like to dedicate my life to helping others and Casa Hogar Los Angelitos. This is my real dream, because I want other children to have the opportunity to grow, to live, and to receive love and education so that they can break the chains of poverty.

> He will redeem them from oppression and violence, for their lives are precious to Him.
> —*Psalms 72:14*

Today, Ricardo is in his last internship period to receive a degree as an architect. He returns to help with design and ideas for the new Casa Hogar Educational and Art Center, wanting to create opportunity for other young people to have a future with hope.

The Slagg Family

In many ways, Mexico reminds me of the rural part of Texas where I grew up—the mix of property uses, the defiant right to live your life and do with your property as you choose.

In my old neighborhood, there were a few nice homes, some old dilapidated homes, commercial buildings, wrecked cars, and vacant land—and just down the road lived the Slagg family. They had a little farm with pigs, mules, cows, chickens, and a large vegetable garden. The house was quite small with a lot of people living all together. It didn't seem very well maintained, and I doubt if it had ever been painted.

Every day, our school bus would stop in front of the Slagg farm. I always saved a seat for the oldest daughter, Opal. Although she was almost three years older than me, she was in my class at school.

There were five Slaggs in school. The oldest was Harold, a handsome young man (at least I thought so) who was older than the others in his class and who was a friend of my older brother's. Harold dropped out of school before graduating, because he was needed to work the farm with his family. Plus, it's really difficult to continue in school when you are a lot older than everyone else in class.

Sometimes I got off the bus with Opal at their house and then walked home from there. The farm was owned by an uncle who had immigrated from some European country and spoke with a heavy accent—but he was the owner, and the rest of the family worked the farm for him and lived there at his pleasure. No one in the family talked much—they kept to themselves, except

Harold, who used to visit and go possum or rabbit hunting with my brother.

I don't remember how I knew that the uncle was molesting one of the younger daughters—but I knew. Opal married as soon as she graduated from 6th grade. Harold, who always seemed slightly embarrassed about his family, also left home as soon as he could.

Traveling to the migrant farm camps outside Manzanillo during the season is an eye-opening and somewhat depressing adventure. Located just kilometers from modern housing and facilities, we find immigrants mostly from the southern states of Mexico living under plastic tarps with *palos* (sticks) holding up the plastic, protecting them to a small extent from the downpour of rains and blistering heat of the sun. They had cardboard on the floor for mats and a few wooden crates for tables and storage.Usually there's no running water (other than ditch or irrigation water), bathroom facilities, or a good way to wash clothes and body. It is a level of poverty that would match any place in the world.

Throughout the years, we have tried to provide food, clothing, and medical help and offer families the opportunity of education for their children. It took a long time for most of the groups to trust us enough to accept help. Now, they will usually accept the food and clothing and sometimes medical help, but rarely do they accept help with education for their children.

I think the resistance to education is twofold: fear of the unknown and fear that if the children become "too educated," they might choose to leave this hard life and the family behind. Family survival and way of life is dependent on maintaining the family unit together with each one contributing their "fair" share.

A number of years ago, we were in the state of Guerrero outside the municipality of Tecuanapa. The local church asked us to visit a family in desperate need. The church had been helping them, but they had concerns about the children. Guiber, Lupita, and I went to where they were living—or I should say 'barely existing.' The mother had passed away two years before during childbirth. There were four children in the family. The oldest was a twelve-year-old girl who had inherited the responsibility of the mother, and the youngest was a two-year-old baby.

As we drove up in our nice van, it was a shocking scene. The family was eating tortillas that had been cooked over a wood fire and living under a shedlike cover in what was *literally* a pig sty. *They were living with the pigs!*

The two-year-old baby was crawling around in the dirt, without diaper or any other protection. The father, who looked to be about fifty, was sitting on the dirt floor, and the oldest daughter was bringing him his tortillas as she finished cooking them. It was a scene that is hard to imagine could exist in today's world.

We stood because there was no place to sit except the dirt floor, and we talked with the father and the oldest daughter for about thirty minutes.

We had brought some bulk food (beans and rice) and some secondhand clothing that we thought they could use. In reality, I don't know how they would even be able to cook the beans or rice, and the clothing would just be piled in the corner with the few other items they owned.

Our main goal was to encourage him to let us take the children back to Manzanillo to the casa hogar so we could take care of them and put them in school. We offered to help him, and the church was willing to help him find a place to live. In the end, he indicated he was content with his life and didn't need any help except food. And when we tried to persuade him to let us help the children, his comment was "What would *I* do if they were not here to take care of *me*?"

I was concerned about a family in one of the migrant camps outside of Manzanillo. A very thin young girl who looked to be about 11 was showing to be about seven or eight months pregnant. Sometimes the stomachs can be quite swollen because of *amebas*, extreme malnutrition, or liver disease. However, I was pretty sure this little girl was pregnant. She lived with the rest of her family in their tarp protection, and I suspected that her father or other family member was also the father of her baby.

I had met a doctor with the social security hospital that was willing to go out with me to check the girl. I was hoping that perhaps he could provide medical help through the social security program. Apparently I had not sufficiently prepared him for what he would see. When we arrived at the camp, he just sat in the van, stunned, looking straight ahead and refusing to get out.

Even though this camp was similar to many other camps (throughout the area all together populated by several thousand migrants) set up in close proximity to modern housing and facilities, this doctor said he had no idea that there were people existing like this.

He was very angry, and when I finally persuaded him to get out of the van, he started yelling at the leader of the migrants. *"How can you let this kind of situation exist?"*

I imagine that once we left, he put that scene into a closed compartment in his mind. He never came back, and he never moved a finger to help find a solution. I am sure he was embarrassed that this situation existed right under his nose, and probably, like the grumpy lady in Limerick, he was angry that he had been confronted by the reality of it.

Ireland, Texas, Mexico—so very different, but like most places in this world, similar in so many ways.

The prevailing attitudes in many countries give priority to the rights of the parents over the rights of the children. It is a general, unspoken philosophy that parents, as creators and "owners" of their children, instinctively know what's best for their child, will do what is best for their child, have the responsibility to care for their child and that child should be with its parent(s), regardless. If a child is born into extreme poverty, prostitution, or a family that makes their living from pornography or drugs, that is their fate in life. Most social service agencies might temporarily remove a child from a dangerous or abusive situation, but many times at the first opportunity, that child is returned to the same negative environment he or she came from.

What weight should be given to the child and his future when the rights of the parents are in conflict with the future safety and rights of the child? To take into consideration that "children are people, not property, and have the right to be protected, cared for and treated with respect."

Mexico has very strong children's rights laws.

> The Mexican Constitution provides that the State has the duty to promote respect for the dignity of all children and the full exercise of their rights. It also provides that children have the right to satisfy their nutritional, health, educational, and recreational needs. Several laws have been enacted in order to implement this mandate, most importantly the federal Law on the Protection of the Rights of Children and Adolescents. In addition, Mexico is a signatory to several treaties that impact children's rights.
>
> —www.LOC.gov

However, it is not always easy or financially feasible to make sure that the rights of children can be protected. It also depends on who has the responsibility of making sure those rights are honored. Generally, it is the parent or caretaker. However, if that caretaker is abusive or ignorant of those rights or incapable of providing the nutritional, educational or recreational needs, then what? Knowing that Mexico has laws to protect children makes it even more important to take advantage of that to take action on behalf of the children.

When a family comes in to the casa hogar, one of the first things we do is help the eldest child find childhood again. Usually, especially if a girl, she has been given the heavy responsibility of being the parent. There is little room for fun or play or caring for themselves. They usually come very burdened and sad, even as young as seven, eight, or nine. Such was Brenda's situation.

Brenda and the Indy 500

One recent Memorial Day weekend, I found myself watching all the major events of the day. Normally, I like to think I am too busy preparing meals and entertaining to sit and watch television.

Because it was Memorial Day, I had bought flowers to take to the cemetery, but then I decided not to go. I didn't like to think of my son, my sister, my mother, and other loved ones buried in the ground, and I hoped that if they were watching, they would understand.

In my family, Memorial Day weekend is about remembering those who are gone. In Mexico during Mexico's Memorial Day (All Saints Day), you can buy loaves of bread shaped like a

Nine-year-old Brenda.

body—well sort of a puffy funny body—that is supposed to represent a loved one who is gone. Favorite foods are prepared and taken to the cemetery where everyone eats, laughs, cries, and remembers. A mini-party is held that spiritually includes the deceased family member(s). In the U.S., we "remember" by eating—hamburgers, hot dogs, brats, homemade ice cream, cakes, pies—and watching parades and sports. I'm not sure how that benefits the dead, but perhaps that is how we make ourselves feel better.

Still unable to begin anything productive, like cooking or cleaning, I started watching the Indy 500. My eight-year-old granddaughter asked me, "Mimi, what is the Indy 500?"

For those who didn't grow up watching the Memorial Day parades, ceremonies, and "Gentlemen, Start Your Engines!" on Memorial Day, the Indy 500 is an American national spectacle—a 500-mile race in one stadium that takes place each year in Indianapolis, Indiana. Tears well up in the eyes of many as the song *Back Home In Indiana* is sung, and the drivers all line up, eager to make their name in history. I noticed that this year the terminology was changed and "Gentlemen, start your engines" became "Drivers, start your engines" because a woman had joined the ranks of qualifying drivers.

I grew up in Houston where A. J. Foyt was king, winning the Indianapolis 500 *four times...* the first ever to do so. What his determination and those wins did was to show those who followed in his footsteps that it could be done. His success became the measure for all the drivers who came after him—as did Brenda's success.

Brenda came from a small fishing village south of Manzanillo. She was part of a family living in extreme poverty, existing together in a two-room house with a great-grandmother, grandmother, aunts, and cousins. When Brenda was seven, their mother abandoned her husband

and family, leaving Brenda with the responsibility to help care for her four younger siblings. They were in extreme circumstances.

Through a government agency of the state, Brenda arrived at Casa Hogar Los Angelitos at the tender age of eight along with Graciela, Pancho, Raul, and the youngest sister, Laura, who was younger than two years old.

While little Pancho was throwing rocks at the wall in anger during those first few weeks, Brenda was crying every night for her mother, clutching a little stuffed bear that had been given to her, feeling alone and lost.

Little by little, Brenda began to adjust, and with tutoring she became one of the top students in her class. When it was time for her *quinceañero* (a coming-of-age tradition in Mexico to celebrate a girl's fifteenth birthday), I was hoping she would *not* decide to leave and go back to her family. (Throughout the early years of the casa hogar, the magic age for each child to leave was between twelve and fifteen years.)

At fifteen, the girls thought they were ready to find a *novio* (sweetheart) and start a family, generally without the benefit of marriage (which seems to be a luxury) and the boys expected to go to work supporting themselves and any existing family they might have.

It's hard for me to be judgmental about this practice, because that's the way it has been for hundreds of years. It was that way one hundred years ago when my grandmother finished the sixth grade, married at fifteen and had a baby at sixteen. My mother didn't do much different. She dropped out of school, married at sixteen, and had her first child when she was seventeen. However, things are different now. If you don't have a minimum of a high school education, it is extremely difficult to get a job that provides a good income. Daily existence becomes the most success that many can expect.

During the first years of the casa hogar, graduating from sixth grade was the marker. A mother, grandmother, or other family member would come to claim the now "adult" child. They were educated *enough*, old *enough* to work, and should begin contributing to the family. This was how the family worked. Like Opal from the little farm down the road. She graduated from the 6th grade, and it was time for her to become an adult.

It was discouraging to watch each child leave the casa hogar and leave behind their potential for success. The custom was set, and breaking that custom meant changing the mentality and the "marker."

When Brenda's father came and said he had decided to take the children out of the casa hogar because it was too difficult for him to visit, my heart sank. I was frantically trying to think of a way to handle this situation.

If a parent or family member comes with real intent to pull their child out of the casa hogar, there is not much we can do to prevent it.

Not wanting to send these children back to the life they would have gone back to, I came up with a plan. I liked Brenda's father and thought he seemed like a decent man—just very poor and without any opportunity to change his life.

I asked him, "Why don't you move to Manzanillo, where you can be closer to your children? Perhaps we can hire you to help us with maintenance and help you to find housing that you can afford."

I asked him if he knew how to drive...no, he had never driven. I asked if he knew how to read and write. No, he had never had the opportunity to go to school. So in order to save his five children, I felt we first had to save the father. We set him up in a little place close to the casa hogar, enrolled him in an adult education school just a couple of blocks away, and by the end of six months had him enrolled in a driver's education class. Within a year, he had graduated with a sixth-grade equivalency and had earned his drivers license. By the end of the first year, he had saved enough money to buy an old pickup and had found a job as maintenance man for one of the larger hotels. *Now* the children also had a chance.

Brenda continued in school and became the first to graduate from high school, the first to enter university, and first to graduate—Brenda is now a Doctor of Orthodontics.

She was the first child we had cared for who continued with her education past junior high school. When it was time for her to begin the application process for college, she was hesitant to apply to any college. She never dreamed that this was a possibility for her. She took the first step—deciding what she wanted to study—and then she made her first application.

We wanted her to go to the University of Colima because of the proximity to the casa hogar and the cost savings. Although her grade point average was 9.4 (very high), she was not accepted at the state school. Ready to give up, we said, "No, you can't give up! What other school offers the same career? University of Guadalajara—but it seemed quite expensive for the career she wanted. What other? Morelia!

The University of Morelia offered the career she was looking for. But Morelia, in Michoacan? Where the drug cartels were in control of many of the mountain areas and active in most of the state? Not my choice for her! However, she made up her mind, she was going to do it.

Brenda made the application and was accepted. It took approximately six years and unbelievable commitment. She survived robberies, fear to go out after dark and had more than several hospital overnights as a result of high stress. Every three months Brenda would take the 10-hour bus ride from Morelia to Manzanillo to check in and maintain contact.

She began to make friends with both students and professors, but never told anyone that she was from a casa hogar. She felt that if they knew, they would treat her differently, reject her. Finally, once she proved herself and developed more confidence, she began to let her close friends know more about who she was and where she had come from. They were amazed, because it is very difficult, if not impossible, for a person who comes from a casa hogar or from extreme poverty to ever make it to the level Brenda had achieved. That is not their fate. The cost alone is prohibitive—only the middle or upper class could dream to be a doctor.

Brenda had made the decision, had the determination, and we made the decision to financially support her efforts. It was not only an investment in Brenda's future, but an investment in the future of all the other children who would dare to dream and follow in her footsteps. She led the way, and through her determination to succeed she encouraged all those who came after her. Andrés, Artemio, Laura, Graciela, Julio, Juan, Annabel, Ricardo, and so on.

As I continued to watch the Indy 500 with cars roaring round and round the track for 500 miles traveling at speeds of 200 miles per hour and more, it was very clear that the goal of the race now was to win, at all cost.

For some, just to qualify to enter the race and get to the finish line had been enough. 500 miles of turns, trials, accidents, blow ups...one mistake, one wrong move could loose the race, cause damage or even death.

You have to be alert, focused, and stay the course. You have to refuel, check your tires and if you loose your confidence or move in fear you will make mistakes. Others will try to knock you out of the race, pass you, cut you off, even sabotage your car. You can go faster than everyone else, but if you crash or run out of gas, but if you don't make it to the finish line, you don't win.

I kept drifting into thoughts about life being like a race and feeling rather depressed about my age and the race I am in being almost over. I was thinking about the future of the casa hogar and how it has been like a long-distance race—the endurance has taken its toll, and I wondered out loud, *"How much further can I run?"*

Paul the Apostle said,

> Let us run with patience the race that is set before us.
>
> —*Hebrews 12:1*

So perhaps that is my answer: patience.

I'm not an ardent fan of any sport, but I do like the people part. I like the personal stories, and like many I will watch the preshow hype—the emotion, the excitement, and in this case, I was interested in the drivers' interviews. Each driver was determined and focused on winning. This year I was particularly interested in the histories and profiles of some of the drivers.

Sometimes the most unlikely person finishes first. Like the Australian, Will Power.

in 2018, he won the Indy 500. He had never even raced in the Indy 500 before and he was older than some of the other drivers—so his win was unexpected. He had worked hard, put together a great support team, invested in a good vehicle, overcame wrecks, disappointments, and even a killer bee attack! He drove the race with confidence, calm, and a belief that he could do it. He dared to dream and in the end he found his place with other racing greats, Foyt, Unser, Mears.

We could easily rename Dr. Brenda: Dr. Will Power! Because like the Australian Will Power, she had to battle the course to get to the finish line, leading the way, staying focused, determined and exuding tremendous *willpower*. Because she dared to dream, others also found the courage to dream and to follow that dream.

> Call unto me and I will answer you and show you great and mighty things (things you never imagined).
>
> —*Jeremiah 33:3*

I See You!

> You have to look people in the eye and let them know you see who they are before they'll listen to you.
>
> —*Rachel Phifer,* The Language of Sparrows

    Our eyes see, and then we process based on our own lives, environment, and experiences. Beauty is seen differently through the different eyes and perceptions of the beholder. It is said that all things have beauty, but in order to recognize the beauty, our hearts, minds, and eyes must be able to "see" that beauty. Many times, we see only what we are trained to see.

    There's an expression in some cultures that conveys a deeper meaning when a person truly recognizes or connects to another person. To see someone's heart, and see who that person is beneath their name, skin, size, or other exterernal feature, and to simply say "I see you."

If you saw the movie *Avatar* you would have seen the tender moment when *Neytiri*, the indigenous woman, expressed her love for Jake Sully by saying, simply and tenderly, "I see you, Jake Sully."

In the Eastern tradition of yoga, each person is greeted *"Namaste." I bow to you, I recognize you, I see you.*

I met a Lakota Sioux man during a book signing at our gallery many years ago—Dr. A. C. Ross, also known as *Ehanamani* (Walks Among). He has written a number of books, but one of his most popular books is *Mitakuye Oyasin* describing the strong connections of the major Native American tribes to the different peoples and cultures of the world.

Mitakuye Oyasin—We are All Related honors each individual and the sacredness of life, as understood by the Lakota Sioux. *I see you, I know you because we are all one.*

My grandmother, whose mother was referred to as a "half-breed" when she was a child, usually turned her head slightly to the left when a photo was taken of her, so that her eyes were never full front. Many indigenous people throughout the world will not allow a photo to be taken that shows their eyes. To look into the eyes of another person is to see or capture the very soul of that person.

When Dave and I first started going to Mexico, I had my favorite beach vendors...Pedro from Guerrero, Pablo from Oaxaca, Lupita from Guerrero, etc. Many times I would take cookies, water, or a sandwich out for them as they would show me their wares. Even though I couldn't speak Spanish much more than *taco, gracias,* and a few other key words (which I've been told I always said with a Texas accent), we found a way to communicate.

Pedro, came walking up onto our yard one hot afternoon with a blanket and handed it to me. He was still looking thin and weakened after the malaria he had suffered in the mountains of Guerrero. In my broken Spanish, I said, "Oh, Pedro thank you so much, but I can't buy a blanket today."

He placed it in front of me and said, "No it's a gift."

"But why, Pedro?" (A gift of a blanket is worth a lot to a hungry young man from Guerrero.)

He quietly and haltingly said, "I want to give you this gift...because you treat me like a person...you see me."

It still chokes me up to think how he must have felt to live in a world where for many he didn't exist, where people looked at him but didn't really see him as a person.

I used to smile at the little boys on the street when they jumped up on the running board of the car to wash the windows for a few pesos. Like most tourists, I thought, "Aren't they cute" or "Poor little things" then felt good as I gave them a couple of pesos.

Whether on the hot beach or on the streets, it seemed all the smiles and personalities had the same sweet enthusiasm. But I never thought about what they might be going back to, what their lives were like, or how they had to live.

When my son died in 1994, everything changed for me...for both Dave and me...and it became the beginning of a different life. My heart was broken and my spirit raw. I was ready to die myself, and my grief was inconsolable. During the months that followed, I believe that God opened doors for me that literally saved my life. My life and focus totally changed during that time, and I felt called to make a difference in the lives of the children in Mexico. I was determined to follow that call. (The details of that part of my life and calling are covered in more detail in the book *Each Day a Portion.*)

With little knowledge of what we were doing we began a food program in 1995, feeding street children in Manzanillo. Then opened the doors of Casa Hogar Los Angelitos, a full time facility, in 1996. It was during those early years that my eyes were opened and I began to really see...I began to see the pain behind the smiles, the horror that so many children, vendors, and street people went back to at the end of the day.

I suddenly saw the beach vendors and the boys who jumped up on our running board to wash our car windows very differently.

Through my son's death, God changed the direction of our lives, and because of that, He also has changed the direction of the lives of thousands of children. The ripple of help spreads from there.

Why is it that people like Pedro, indigenous to a land, living in poverty, are treated as if they aren't part of our world? Could it be because we are afraid that we might see our own selves? If we look closely enough, we might recognize that, regardless of where Pedro was born or the color of his skin, we are all equal in God's eyes. As the Lakota Sioux say, "We are all related." Perhaps we think to ourselves, "He can't possibly be related or equal to me!" But it's difficult to maintain a superior image of ourselves if we come face to face with the concept that we are all related or that we are all equal in God's eyes, regardless of money, beauty, color, or birth.

The new DNA tests from *ancestry.com* and such programs as *23 and Me* have changed many preconceived ideas we had about who we are and where we come from. I, an "Irish" redhead, have recently discovered that I have a number of third and fourth cousins of African descent and some who are Ashkenazi Jews. On the other side, many of my relatives are outlaws and renegades. Truthfully, I find that to be rather exciting, and at least to me, it proves my point that we are all related.

Throughout the years, I have remembered my friend Pedro from Guerrero. Some of you who have been to Manzanillo may have met Pedro—he is now a man with a grown family and a stall at the Tianguis market in Santiago. I always try to stop and say hello to him when I am there, but mostly I remember what he said to me. It was a seemingly small thing, but my friend Pedro showed me how important it is to treat each person—no matter who they are, where they come from, or their situation in life—as an individual and to let them know that I recognize them as a person and that I actually *see* them!

Most of the children at CHLA come from generational poverty and many from indigenous families. The "Pedro" concept of really seeing each child has become one of the basics of Casa Hogar Los Angelitos's philosophy. Once a child enters CHLA, they become part of a family, a home, a future. They have value, and they learn that someone sees them and cares about them.

I have observed that all these children seem naturally beautiful, bright, talented, and they have the same emotions, hopes, and dreams that children from every where in the world have. They just need the opportunity to blossom.

Regardless of where each child comes from, they all have a powerful and unique story. My hope is that I can tell a few of their stories in a way that touches hearts, and you will see that child and others in a different light. I hope you can say to yourself and whisper to that child, "I see your heart, your fear, your determination...I SEE you, and I care!"

This past year, Dave and I joined some of our family on a river cruise. This was not our first cruise, and while each cruise is different scenery, guests, ships, everything...there is one consistency. From the chef to the housekeeper they all learn your name and greet you by name beginning the first day you arrive on the boat. At first I thought wow, that is really amazing! Now I take it for granted that it is part of their job, to learn the names of the guests they have contact with. It is part of the ambiance that makes each guest feel special and welcome, not just another body to be taken care of. By the end of the trip, you feel you are friends—calling each other by your first names.

When a family of five from Jalisco was brought in to the casa hogar I was in Colorado.

However, I always receive the reports of each child when they come in, and I look at the profiles and history. When I met those five for the first time, welcoming them to their new home, the oldest boy defiantly looked at me and said, a bit defiantly, "I bet you don't even know my name!" He was standing next to his younger brother and gave him a knowing look and smile.

I had looked at their names just before I went to meet them, so I smiled at him and said, "Of course I know your name." To the oldest boy I said, "You are Cesar, and you" (to the younger brother) "are Cristian." Both looked surprised, and that small gesture of knowing their names when I met them made all the difference in the way they began to respond in their new home. They were important enough for someone to know their name. Watching the reaction of those boys had an effect on me as well.

There are things, sometimes simple things, that we remember from childhood that make a big difference in the way we perceive ourselves. I always felt rather ugly, with a face full of freckles and barely enough strawberry-colored hair to cover my head, but every time I walked into the education building at church where my Sunday School class was located, a beautiful lady named Naomi Cotton would greet me by name and say something special about me or my dress. She always looked at me and smiled. I felt like she saw me with loving eyes, and her attention made me feel special.

There is something important about the connection between a person's name and how that person feels about themself. Perhaps that is why we have nicknames that tell others more about us: El Chapo, (Shorty), Junior, etc. My great-grandfather was called "Bone" Hogan, perhaps because he was quite tall and lanky, or perhaps because one of the many things he did was to lead hunting trips and process wild game or cattle for people. A lot of bones involved there. Regardless, it was what everyone affectionately knew him by—"Bone" or "Uncle Bone."

Most people name a baby when it is born, but at a certain age, some cultures give them another name—an adult name—more specific to their personality or spirit, specific to who they are and will become—a serious, thoughtful name...I personally like "Dances With Wolves." However, I did one of those internet tests that tell you what your Native American name would be (based on answers I gave to their 'canned' questions that I don't remember) and mine didn't come up Dances with Wolves. My "native American" name was "Gives Food to Wolves"—not as exciting, but fitting, somehow. But *much* better than what some rude people used to call me: "Carrot Top," "Pinky Puss," or "Red."

Cruel names can have a very negative effect on the self-esteem of a child. How I hated those names!

Of course, there is the other side of the coin—when people take pride in an affectionately funny or negative name. "Big Jim" Hogg, famous governor of Texas in the late 1800s, carried his undignified name proudly. He stood over six feet tall and weighed in at 300 pounds. His name is still a household word for the old timers in Texas. When he shockingly named his only daughter *Ima*, people didn't dare make fun of the lovely young woman who became the "shining star" of Texas. Understandably, it did inspire many jokes, including adding a nonexistent sister, "Ura." So through the years the story evolved that Governor Hogg had *two* daughters, Ima Hogg and Ura Hogg.

I'm sure many people wondered: Did he name his daughter *Ima* just to prove he could? Surely he must have realized how it would sound even a hundred years later. However, Miss Ima Hogg never married, and she carried her name with the dignity befitting a famous socialite and Texas 'royalty.'

When people called me "Red," it made me think of an ugly, brutish, red-haired thug that everyone called "Red." He was really ugly! I didn't want to be associated with *that* name.

As I pass each child at the casa hogar or talk with them, I try to smile, touch their head or shoulder, make eye contact and call them by name to connect with them so that they feel special. *You have value to me. You are someone.* For me, they are each very special, and I want them to feel the way Ms. Cotton made me feel.

One day I decided to sit in the play area with a couple of the little girls. They were laughing and giggling about everything. I loved watching their faces and laughter. Then Briana, a five year old, laughed as she pointed to the "aging" sag beneath my chin and laughingly said, "Iguana!" Responding with the same giggles, little Kasandra said "Sí, iguana!" I put an incredulous look on my face and said, "IGUANA!? ***IGUANA***!!!?"

"Sí iguana!" and they laughed even harder. Well, even though I *do not* think I have a neck like an iguana, their innocent laughter was so infectious that I had to laugh, too.

I would like to think that perhaps they were trying to make me feel special, although I think they could have chosen a more sensitive way to do that. If you think about it, however, there are some really spectacular-looking iguanas! I went home, and when I was all alone, I looked in the mirror just to see what they were talking about. Children can be so brutal in their honesty.

I grew up in a time when the expression "Children should be seen and not heard!" was common and firmly believed. Sometimes I can understand that better than other times.

The proud iguana.

I think children of poverty evoke an emotion that many of us don't want to feel. It's called *compassion*.

In Matthew 20:34, the Bible refers to this feeling:

> Jesus had compassion on them and touched their eyes. Immediately they received their sight and followed him.
>
> —*Matthew 20:34, NET*

His compassion precipitated action.

When I first saw the little boys in the streets washing car windows or spewing diesel from their mouths and deftly lighting it, I felt 'pity.'

"Poor little things!" I felt sorry for them. But I kept going, and didn't think of them again.

However, when I began working with some of those children and really seeing them up close, it changed my heart. Seeing beneath their enthusiastic smiles and personalities, my pity changed to compassion.

While there is a relationship between pity and compassion, they are not the same. When we feel pity, it doesn't necessarily prompt action. Compassion is different. Compassion gives us the ability to take the perspective of and feel empathy with another person and

I do not *think I look like an iguana!*

stirs the desire to help—to take action in some way.

Too many times the voices of children are unheard, their stories untold, because we don't want the responsibility that might evolve from actually seeing them and allowing ourselves the feeling of compassion.

I Knew You Even Before You Were Born

The Bible tells us that each person is special to God and that He knew us even before we were born! When children can believe they are special to God—even before they were born—that helps give a sense of value to their lives.

> I knew you before I formed you in your mother's womb. Before you were born I set you apart...
> —*Jeremiah 1:5 NLT*

I believed that about my own life, and I have held onto that belief throughout the years.

My older brother and I were raised by our grandparents, while my mother lived next door.

In what could have been an emotionally or socially uncomfortable situation, I don't think my brother and I ever considered that our mother didn't love us. However, during a difficult time in my brother's life, I remember him saying, "If your mother can't love you, who can?"

After all, if you can't trust your mother or your family to protect and care for you, who can you trust? For some reason, as I was growing up, I always felt that I was loved by God. That has given me courage in difficult times and security when I felt abandoned or alone. I felt that even though I might be misunderstood or invisible to others, God could see my heart…He could see me and He knew my name. He knew who I was, and He loved me.

When a child is born, they are born vulnerable with a natural need to trust…they trust their mother or caretaker completely. However, when a child does not have his basic needs met—is not held or loved, is emotionally or physically abandoned, abused or neglected—he quickly learns *not* to trust. He begins to build a protective shield around himself, pushing his emotions deep into his soul, into his cellular development. He builds a shield for protection from hurt and that prevents him from sharing or receiving love. Studies have proven that babies can die when their basic need for touch and security or a sense of love is not met for extended periods.

Every child has the right to feel they are loved by someone, that they belong somewhere, and that there is someone they can trust. This is one of the reasons gang membership is so appealing to young people and why the gangs have so much power over their members: they fill the craving to *belong*, they provide a place of acceptance, and you trust in the group to defend you—to "have your back."

If we can give each child that sense of security, that confidence to believe that they are loved, the sense that God can see their heart and that He knows them by name; then we have given them a gift that can change their lives forever.

My brother and I had each other's backs, and I held onto him for dear life. Our father died when I was six months old, so I never knew him, but as a child, when I felt frustrated or hurt, I would lie on my bed at night and talk to my father. I felt I knew him, even if I had never really known him. I felt that he knew me, even though he was not there. I felt he could see my heart and see my hurt. I would say to myself, "If my father were alive, he wouldn't let that happen to me. He would protect me." I would imagine that I could hear him gently say "I see you—I care." I wanted to believe there was someone who really cared about me, even if he was no longer alive. These thoughts were part of my mechanism to survive as I was growing up. I believe that every child needs that sense of

My brother was my protector.

security, and if it can't be your mother or father, then who?

In 2012, as I wrote *Each Day a Portion,* I didn't know the reality of who my father's biological parents were. I had carried that emotional need since childhood. I wanted/needed to know more about him. Who was he? Where did he come from? What were the circumstances of his birth?

Several years ago I met a man who was introduced to me as someone who had been a good friend of my father's when they were young men together. Normally I am very good at maintaining my composure, but when he was introduced to me, I broke down and could barely talk. Tears were streaming down my face. To meet someone who knew my father and had been friends with him! I was overwhelmed with emotion. Here was a real, human connection. He invited me to his home, and I recorded his voice as he told me stories about my father. As I was leaving, he said something to me that still bothers me. He said, "I go to that cemetery often, and I just don't understand why no one has ever put a marker on his grave."

I felt so sad for the memory of my father. Why didn't someone care enough to put a marker on his grave? To write his name in memorial? His wife (my mother), his mother, family, someone! Everyone should have someone who cares enough to remember them in death. I went to the cemetery that afternoon, walked to where his unmarked grave was, and made arrangements to put a memorial marker on his grave. I wanted him to know "I remember you were here, and even if you are gone, in my heart, in my thoughts, I see you." How could he have lived and died and no one even bothered to remember him?

When my son died there was no relief...even though my heart and spirit wept silently, they cried out in such pain that I could hear them screaming loudly in my mind.

When I visit my son's grave, I can't bear to think of him being buried. Perhaps that's why no one ever put a marker on my fathers grave—it was a physical reminder that he had existed and that he had died.

In the last 5 years, thanks to more DNA studies and research, I have discovered and confirmed what I had suspected for a number of years. My father's father was the only son of my "Granny"—but my father's *mother* was actually a young (12-year-old) girl who lived with my grandparents. It was an old story even then. So many times when a child born "out of wedlock" was a shame to the whole family. Often, the grandmother or another adult woman in the family would disappear for awhile and then came back with a baby. We see this kind of coverup in Mexico, and it is usually the father, stepfather, older brother, or uncle who is the father. The family keeps the child and the secret, never admitting the true paternal responsibility.

I knew my father's father, and even as a child, I didn't like him very much. As I think back, he never showed any interest in my brother or me, and probably thought that his ugly family secret followed him to the grave.

Many of our children have come from situations of prostitution (or, more politely, a "mother with multiple partners") or a situation of abandonment. Some may know who their father was, many do not. But human nature seems to create a desire in all of us to know who our parents are—to know our father, to feel that sense of belonging and connection that comes from believing that our father knows us, wherever he might be, and that he sees us and loves us. Not every child finds that.

We see in the situation of Julio.

Julio

After the storm comes calm.

Dear reader,

I hope this story will be inspirational and a blessing for your life, and you can see that God makes great things and even in this time He is still transforming lives.

—Julio M.

Who am I?

I was born in the city of Mexicali in the state of Baja California on April 10 of the year 2000. I was born a product of sexual abuse by who in reality was also my grandfather. When he realized that my mother was pregnant with me, he tried to make it impossible for me to be born. He gathered medications that my mother should not take during her pregnancy and gave those to her. Apparently the medications had no effect and did not cause me to be aborted, now making me realize that the hand of God was always present, even when I was in the belly of my mother, and that He was always keeping my life safe and is still doing that today. Shortly after I was born, my father, being a violent and aggressive man, hit my mother even while I was in her arms, giving the clear impression to my mother that my life was not worth anything to him, and she realized that he could kill me.

My mother grabbed all my documents, some clothes and ran away to the house of my aunt. During that time my mother was working as a house keeper to get enough money to come to Manzanillo. As soon as she had money and the opportunity we left.

Shortly after arriving in Manzanillo, my mother was with another man, who at first seemed to be quiet and normal—but it was not like that. He began to humiliate and insult my mother, and when he became drunk, he would hit my mother. I was 3 years old at that time, and my brother Andrés was only 1 year old.

Three years later, twins were born: Vanessa and Alberto. My mother seemed marked by men, by rejection, and other issues such as drugs and alcoholism. I did not understand many things, and little by little my heart began to harden because of all the situations that marked my childhood.

When I turned 8 years old, my mother seemed immersed in terrible despair and anguish. During that time my stepfather was not supporting us with economic sustenance, and we were no longer 2 children but 4. It was very hard for my mother to keep 4 children without help.

One day my mother thought of the idea to give me away as if I were an object or something for the benefit of other people who were not my family.

My aunt was shocked by the barbarity of what my mother was going to do and decided to open the doors of her home and heart to support me. For one year, I lived with my aunt and uncle. For me, that year was a blessing, and I always keep it as a treasure within my heart.

The emotional circumstance I was in at that time was unpleasant and very sad. I do remember when I lived with them they bought me all a child would like to have—a spinning top and coloring books. About a month before December arrived, they asked me, "Julio, what gift do you want for Christmas?" I didn't know—I was so excited and happy for that question. I had never been asked that question before! I asked for a computer, although I knew that gift was never going to happen, and in those moments I was so happy that I didn't think about being alone.

Honestly, with the passage of the years and as I learned what my mother had done, I felt like

Above: Julio after he entered the casa hogar.
Below: Julio at his high school graduation.

Joseph (the son of Jacob), who was sold by his brothers to some foreigners; in this case, I was not sold but given away, as if I were an object with no value.

So I was now 9 years old, and bad things seemed to have no end. I felt a despair and an anguish so strong inside me.

I went back to live with my mother when she went to work, and she left me to take care of my two younger brothers and my sister. In reality, I wonder why you would put a young child in charge of his other siblings. I watched my mother leave for work, and then I went out to the street and left my little brothers and sister alone. I came back about an hour before my mother arrived.

During that time on the street, a person began to talk to me about Jesus as a person who loves, forgives, and saves, and he invited me to his church. Since then things started to calm down for me. I remember that I prayed and told Jesus that I wanted to be in a better place and that I wanted to have a better life. He answered my prayer.

Once again my mother gave me away, and I was taken to Casa Hogar Los Angelitos. When I arrived at CHLA, I was almost 10 years old, but the truth is that I felt such quiet peace. I never thought I would ever have support, love, care, and the warmth of a true family home, as I have found here in CHLA.

I have had happy and sad moments. When I arrived here I never believed I would have such a great family and brothers I enjoy and who are like me. I like those moments when I sit in the living room along with other kids and we talk about what it is like to be brothers.

I feel blessed that God put me in a place like CHLA. He has protected me and I believe He will continue to protect me from the many dangers that have become increasingly strong in our society. I thank God for the lives of my Papas, David and Nancy, and I will always be thankful for them, and I will always be grateful to God. Without a doubt, God transforms lives to show the world that He still is doing amazing and wonderful things.

> *Tengo una misión en este mundo, la cual será bendecir y apoyar al mas pequeño, así como Dios lo hizo y lo sigue haciendo conmigo.*
>
> —Julio M.

> *De oídas había oído, más mis ojos ahora ten ven.*
>
> —Job 42: 5

English Translations:

> I have a mission in this world, which will be a blessing to help the smallest, and as God did it, He will keep doing with me.
>
> —Julio M.

> What my ears had heard, my eyes now have seen.
>
> Job 42: 5

Perhaps that is why God took the role of "father to the fatherless." He understands the importance for a child to have that sense of security.

Throughout the years songs have been written about fathers, sad relationships, missing relationships, influential relationships and so on.

Eric Clapton wrote this Grammy-winning song (*My Father's Eyes*) about his father. It is all about the father really seeing his child, loving that child, and that child being able to look back into his father's eyes, and with that he knows…

> Sailing down behind the sun,
> Waiting for my prince to come.
> How will I know him?
> When I look in my father's eyes.
> Feel my heart start to overflow.
> Where do I find the words to say?
> That's when I need my father's eyes.
> Through the distant clouds of tears.
> I'm like a bridge that was washed away;
> My foundations were made of clay.
> As my soul slides down to die.
> How could I lose him?
> What did I try?
> Bit by bit, I've realized
> That he was here with me;
> I looked into my father's eyes

Personally, I like to think I have my fathers' eyes, both my biological father and my heavenly father. I like the way that feels.

Unconditional Love

The most difficult hurts to heal seem to be the emotions that evolve from childhood, usually regarding a mother or father who abandoned you by death, divorce, emotionally through abuse or just disappearing from your life.

As we become adults those hurtful emotions from childhood tend to evolve into anger, jealousy, resentments and we feel that injustice gives us the right to judge the actions of those who have offended us or we put guilt onto ourselves and act out our anger and resentments. Most of the children that come in to the casa hogar feel that they must be guilty of something, or they would not have been abandoned by their parents.

The child who is born into a situation such as Julio's feels as if there is something missing—a hole in his soul that he tries to fill in various ways, sometimes healing, but many times the hole is filled with destructive behavior. Statistics show that many of the cartel members and leaders of gangs and crime fall into that category.

Children that come in to the casa hogar usually have a "missing" or "abusive" father, and because of that, it is difficult for them, especially the boys, who of course tend to look to that *macho* image to feel good about themselves. A child suffering from abuse, neglect, or other traumas doesn't immediately allow themselves to feel love or trust—and we see lots of rocks thrown at the wall out of angry frustration.

Through the "Healing Journey" program we established at Casa Hogar Los Angelitos several years ago, we try to work with each child and help them to replace the traumas of their childhood with a different narrative in order to open their hearts for healing.

When a child enters CHLA, we have a little welcoming ceremony to help that child feel they are part of a family. Regardless of the circumstances they came from—their past traumas or hurts—they are now safe, accepted, and loved for who they are. We refer to that as *unconditional love*.

> When I was a child, I spoke as a child, I understood as a child, I thought as a child: but when I became a man, I put away childish things.
>
> *KJV 1 Corinthians 13:11*

It is not that easy to put away our narratives from childhood and to "put away childish things," especially when it involves our emotional connection with our parents. We have to rewrite our narrative and replace hurt with empathy, trauma with compassion.

In his forward for the book *Each Day a Portion* Dr. Don Phelps wrote; "Linda Sanford found that victims of childhood trauma eventually come to the proverbial fork in the road. Some go on to be survivors while others go down a different path—of violence and self-destruction. The survivors seemed to have found a way to move toward healing by finding a loving relationship that provides consistency, patience, kindness, and hope. Watching Nancy's steadfast love for these boys, I saw how they had transformed and become strong in the broken places. When they entered CHLA years ago, they were diamonds in the rough. That night I saw them sparkle."

We have four Bible verses on the wall in our education center. Verses we put there with the hope of being an inspiration to those who pass through, one of my favorite verses is from Jeremiah.

> For I know the plans I have for you, declares the Lord, plans to prosper you and not to harm you, plans to give you hope and a future.
>
> *Jeremiah 29:11*

It is important that everyone, and especially children feel they have hope for a positive future.

Daniel

It was Saturday before the start of school and the girls from a local beauty school had come to give the first school haircuts.

As I walked onto the scene, there was a mix of emotion in the air. The girls were getting great haircuts and styles...the boys, not so much. It was like a scene at a military camp. How do you get rid of those individual, nonuniform-looking hairstyles? BUZZ CUTS!

Just electric clip all those little pointed or curly styles off. School officials would approve... but the boys were devastated. Truthfully, I was, too. Hair is so important! Take away the hairstyle and you take away some of that sense of individualism. Having a "bad hair day" is a harsh reality that can affect our entire demeanor and self-concept. (Ask me, the little girl who hated her red hair.)

Some of the boys walked past me and wouldn't even look at me. I felt horrible, knowing that they blamed me as well as every other person there for the humiliation they felt.

Little Daniel was nine and according to some, he was *muy profundo*. While you wouldn't think a haircut would matter that much to a nine-year-old, he started running and before anyone could stop him he had climbed up onto the ledge of the second story of the administration office.

Terrified something could happen to him, I took the tough approach. 'Daniel, you come down right now or you are going to be in big trouble!"

Well, *that* didn't work. It just made him more determined *not* to come down.

Then I realized he was starting to cry and he yelled out sobbing, "*Nobody cares about me!!!*"

It was more than I could take, watching this little nine-year-old boy, perched on the ledge above the *palapa*...I started sobbing, too. I walked around to the stairs and climbed to the point where he had climbed up onto the delicate roof of the *palapa* and I held out my hand to him... crying..and I said, "Daniel, I care about you, please come down! I don't want anything to happen to you! I am crying with you because I care so much about you. *Please* take my hand and come down. I promise you will not be punished, but please let me hold you and tell you that I love you!" Even now as I write this I choke up seeing his little face sobbing and crying out in pain, "Nobody cares about me." He was one of those children at the casa hogar who was always getting into trouble. He already understood punishment and criticism; what he didn't understand was love—that someone could care enough about him to share his pain, to really see him...*I see you, Daniel...and I care about you!*

Children like little Daniel, climbing up onto the ledge, are trying to escape their fears and hurts—each day we work with children like Daniel, encourage them, try to give them a sense of belonging. Trust begins to take shape and is re-enforced. But it's not easy to softly break down the hard walls they have constructed around their feelings.

It is important that children understand that their mother's basic love for them cannot be quantified based on her behavior—and it is important for healing that children know that it is okay not to like or even approve of a parent's behavior. They can actually despise the behavior of a mother or father—whether it is abandonment, prostitution, drugs or even abuse—but they don't have to hate the parent. They can love that mother or father while not accepting the behavior. This proves to be emotionally healthier for a child and enables him or her to have an opportunity to forgive and to begin their life-changing behavior.

Remember all the little stones that have cute or special sayings on them—perhaps only a single

Nancy with Daniel and some of his CHLA "brothers."

word—"love" "believe" "hope," etc. It has been and remains a popular gift of remembrance to give to someone, expressing a sentiment or hope. I took a rock and wrote my own saying on it many years ago during a time when I was struggling with some conflicted emotions. I'm sure it has been written by many others before and since.

it simply says, "We like *because*...We love *regardless*." This has been my path throughout life. I may not like what you do, or how you behave, but I can still love you.

Discipline/ Consequences

Punishment has always been a big issue in families and institutions. It seems that "punishment" is either extreme (too severe) or the exact opposite. The ideal goal for "punishment" is more of a balance between the structure of rules and nurturing—to mindfully use discipline as a tool for education, growth, and positive behavior change—not as punishment.

Many times discipline in poverty tends to be negative and more about guilt, penance, and forgiveness than learning and growing. In strongly religious countries, this seems to follow more the early teachings of the Church—guilt, punishment, and forgiveness. However, generally speaking the behavior itself seldom changes.

Punishment can become a form of temporary control or revenge, instead of for education or behavioral change. Along the same line of thinking, the control of children and many times spouses rotates around negative comments or negative innuendos perpetuating the idea that the child/spouse is worthless, bad, and without value outside the immediate circle, thus continuing the cycle of generational poverty.

The most important part of discipline is to remember that discipline is not revenge or payback but it's for the general purpose of educating the child so they can change that behavior. To appropriately do this, it is important to separate the child from the behavior. By separating the child from the behavior, you are able to discipline and reaffirm unconditional love for the child at the same time. The child can then understand that it is the *behavior* that is bad or unacceptable, not the child himself. He learns that even if he messes up he is still loved and has value. For a child who has been abandoned, abused, suffered trauma and has issues of self-esteem and trust, this is very important.

For little Daniel it became important for him to feel that he could trust me and feel the security of that unconditional love.

There are statistics that show that a child in poverty will receive two negative comments for every positive...as compared to children in middle class or more educated families who receive six to twenty positives for every one negative. This is why it is important to be mindful of the comments that we make, intending to approach discipline and situations from a positive perspective.

I believe these observations and comments are so important to the model of CHLA because it is a key ingredient to the approach that can enable us to truly help change the lives of the children who come to us from situations of poverty, abandonment, abuse, and being orphaned. How children are treated, disciplined, encouraged, and helped becomes an important key in healing the damage that risk factors and traumas have caused in their brains. This helps determine how they can eventually move from a "child of fate" without value or hope for the future…to become a "child of great value" with self confidence, and the appropriate life tools to cross out of poverty.

The idea of being in control of life situations and to expect change in others or ones self, even through punishment, doesn't resonate with the general belief that you must accept your fate and the attitude that "I will be able to do this or that, only if God is willing (*si Dios quiere!*) This situation exists because it is God's will, so why try to change the unchangeable, my destiny…that would be false hope." This fixed mentality causes obstacles in changing lives.

The real challenge in a program like CHLA is training and working with teachers and house mothers to convert from the old styles of discipline that they grew up with and to understand this more productive way of discipline and how it works, and to heal their own traumas so that they can be healthy caretakers. We tend to revert to what we know and have experienced when confronted with difficult situations. Training and development has to be ongoing.

The Cartels

Chema was only five when he and his three older brothers came in to the casa hogar. During that time the casa hogar was located in a "storefront" building in Santiago. The front doors were two heavy metal garage doors, exposing the entire down stairs area where the children studied and ate their meals. Chema, the youngest wouldn't stop crying each time his mother came to visit. Benjamin and his older brother Arturo were half-brothers to Chema and Armando. Benjamin and Arturo's biological mother was somewhere in Tecoman, unknown to us. There were three more children (all younger) living with Chema and Armando's mother and father in a lean-to made of sticks at the back of a house on the canal. At one time Chema's father had worked for the local police, but his alcoholism had caused him to lose everything and he spent his life trying to sell ears of corn on the street drinking up any money that he did make. Benjamin and Arturo the older brothers, at 8 and 9 years of age, were sent out each night to hunt for aluminum cans, food and any other valuable item they might find in the dumpsters and trash cans.

These four (Arturo, Benjamin, Armando, and Chema) were brought to us by DIF because of the severe circumstances they were living in, however, when Chema's mother decided to take Chema and Armando back to their lean-to, we couldn't prevent it. She didn't want Benjamin or Arturo because they were not her sons so she left them with us.

During the years that followed, Chema and Armando helped the family by washing car windows on the street, bringing home as much as 300 pesos (close to $15) per week. The family survived on that money. By this time the family had moved to the bull ring, sleeping under the stands and cooking their tortillas on sticks they would gather.

Armando began sniffing glue early, and throughout the years he was in jail more than he was out of jail. Each time he was released you could see him back on the streets washing car windows. Chema tried to find his way, but neither had been able to go to school once they were taken out of the casa hogar, they couldn't read or write, so options were limited.

As Chema reached maturity he was determined to learn to read and write and get a high school diploma through the adult education program. He had a job at a local gym and had hopes of joining the army. However, things were not to work out for Chema. The army wouldn't accept him because he didn't have a high school degree. He worked to get the equivalent of a GED but just didn't have doors open for him.

Now a young man of 23, he had made arrangements to rent a house for himself, his mother, younger siblings, and his little daughter. The area was a quiet area and he had a deal with the man he rented from.

Not long after moving in, he had a visitor (the real owner of the house). "You and your family have to leave. I need this house and if you aren't out by this afternoon when I return, you will be sorry." Chema begged the man in desperation.

"I have no other place to take my family. I need a day to find another place!"

When afternoon came, Chema and his family were still in the house. Arriving as promised, not only the man who claimed to be the owner of the house but also a half dozen other armed men.

It was said that Chema argued with the man before they took him to their vehicle and drove off. Several hours later Chema was dumped on the front yard of the house...dead. He had been

Young Benjamin.

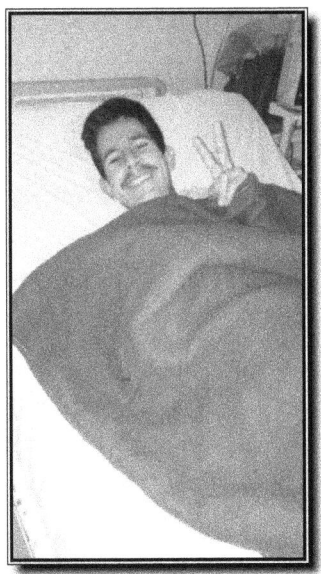

Benjamin awaiting a kidney transplant.

tortured and murdered. It is very probable that Chema had become involved with one of the drug cartels as so many other young men who felt they had limited options did, or just happened to be in the wrong place at the wrong time. We don't know.

Sadly, Chema's older brother, Benjamin, had been sick with kidney failure and had passed away the year before Chema was murdered. He had been on dialysis for over a year waiting for the possibility of a kidney transplant. His body just couldn't hold out, and now one year later... Chema.

In recent years, Mexico has taken some serious public relations hits because of all the cartel activity and negative news. The fear of violence has affected comfort levels for many visitors traveling to and through Mexico. Those of us who spend a great deal of time in Mexico and who work with the local people know that the real violence is between the cartels. Groups fighting for control of the market. In the case of Manzanillo, control of the port and the drugs going in and out.

We watched hundreds of Federal Police (some say thousands) in their black, heavily armored trucks, black face masks, high-powered AK-somethings, and bulletproof vests roll in to

Manzanillo after a surge of violence between several major cartels. That didn't particularly give me a sense of security, but it did let us know that there are serious violent activities taking place to curb some of the other violence. Everyone that was aware of what was going on kept a low profile during that month, avoiding areas where the Federal Police were stationed or congregated.

One night after dance rehearsal at the casa hogar, I took Rodrigo, a former member of the casa hogar who was visiting that evening, to his brother's apartment. The apartment happened to be located in an alley a block away from the casa hogar. We sat in the car for a few minutes talking and I noticed a Federal Police truck go past the end of the alley. Realizing it was already after ten pm I needed to get off the streets and back to the condo, I said good night and drove to the end of the alley.

As I pulled out of the alley, the Federal Police truck pulled in behind me. I was alone, and I thought to myself, *just be cool, take your time, don't look at the police vehicle, pretend you don't notice it*. I kept heading toward home, hoping I wouldn't get pulled over. Finally, I gave a huge sigh of relief as I turned into the side street that leads to our condo and the police truck kept going. I had noticed that our vehicle (a bigger gray Ford Expedition) seemed to encourage a second glance from the police when they passed, and suddenly I realized my vehicle, which we used to haul a lot of people and luggage, was also a popular style and size for a narco car.

Sometimes we make decisions based on need or desire. I made a decision based on fear. Time to get rid of that car and replace it with something a little less narco looking.

When you routinely deal with tough situations, you're not supposed to get angry, but sometimes my blood boils when I think about all the children that we've lost throughout the years…children who were sent back to the despair they had escaped from by the very system that should have protected them.

Jose Ivan left at 15 and was murdered by age 18—a cartel was trying to convince his older brothers to join their organization. Marta went back to her family at 14. She became a prostitute, like her mother, by the age of 15. At 16, she had a baby who died mysteriously. She spent time in a correction institution and was then released. At one time she came to visit, and I remember her saying to me, "Nancy, you cannot even imagine the horrible things I've seen." I don't know what has happened to her since that day.

We took in a young woman we had cared for until she turned 14, when her family took her out. Two years ago, she came to our door begging for help, dragging behind her three little children. We were the only place where she felt she could be secure. The abusive father of her three children was threatening to kill her if she left him. She had nowhere safe to go. We kept her and her children safe and helped her get legal help to move away. This young mother is an example of what happens over and over to those children who leave the safety of a home like CHLA before they are ready and go back into the life they came from.

Several years ago, I went to an event to help support a new and much-needed project to care for abused women—those who are trying to escape from the prison of forced prostitution, drugs, and abuse. The stories are horrendous, and for some people who have not worked with or been aware of this kind of situation (as I have), those stories are unbelievable. While listening to the horrible and painful story that this young woman was recounting, I was so angry I felt faint. The sense of frustration was overwhelming. Too many times our hands are tied by a culture where this happens over and over. As I was listening to her story, a lady from across the table slipped a note to me which simply said, "That is the reason Casa Hogar Los Angelitos exists!"

EXACTLY! That *is* why Casa Hogar Los Angelitos exists! CHLA doesn't care only for poor children. Most of the children we care for come from potentially dangerous situations. If these children were not under our care, for many of them the story of that young woman would be their story or worse. We encourage the children and young people we care for to stay with us, continue their education, and *don't* leave until they are ready to be successful. We are unique in that we don't send them back to the same life they came from when they turn 12, 13, or 14. We know that if they return to the streets their percentages for survival are minimal along with any hope for a decent future.

This young mother is an example of what happens over and over to those children who leave the safety of a home like CHLA before they are ready and go back in to the life they came out of. Yet, many times it is the mentality of our social "child protective" system that children are forced to return to a family member, removed from foster care and programs such as ours, as soon as possible, without regard for the danger involved.

We have had to fight the system in order to continue to care for the children who have grown up in the casa hogar through the completion of their education. We feel it is important for young people to have the opportunity to complete their high school education, vocational training, or career training. Without education, economic and social success is extremely difficult. It is uncommon for children to stay in a facility in Mexico beyond fifteen or sixteen years of age. In the U.S., seventeen or eighteen is the magic number.

Are young people really ready to return to a hostile and dangerous world at the age of 14, 15, 16, or 17 without the benefit or opportunity of continued education?

Child trafficking and prostitution are becoming the biggest businesses in the world, and all these children live at risk of being trapped into that. However, we don't want to kid ourselves and think that this problem is only "south of the border." The U.S. and Canada are at the top of the list as customers for the import of human trafficking, creating a very lucrative business for the exporters and importers!

A couple of weeks ago I stopped at a *kiosko* close to where we live, and there was a little boy standing close to the door asking for money for food. I stopped and talked with him asking about his family, where he lived, did he go to school, etc.

He said that he had another brother and he had a little sister. But his little sister "disappeared" a few months ago, and they don't know what happened to her.

Every week I read or hear about a child disappearing. It is a nightmare that never ends. I told him about the casa hogar and bought him a package of cinnamon rolls. When I gave those to him, his eyes lit up, he quickly said *"gracias"* and took off, opening the package as he was running. I am confident that he would never come to the casa hogar, because his mother and brother need him to help support the family. He will never be able to attend school, and chances are as soon as he is old enough, he will enter into the drug business.

Child trafficking and prostitution are becoming the biggest businesses in the drug world, and all these children live at risk of being trapped into that. Many people kid themselves and think that it is only a "south of the border" problem. On the contrary, the U.S. and Canada are at the top of the list as customers for the victims of human trafficking, creating a very lucrative business for the exporters and importers!

Our first goal at CHLA is to help each child heal physically, emotionally, and spiritually, but sometimes healing isn't enough. Keeping the child until they complete their schooling and supporting them through higher education and considering them part of the casa hogar family even after they become adults is the approach we have found to be most successful.

Pilar

Pilar and her older brother were brought to us when she was 7 and her brother 9. The authorities brought them because their mother was in an unstable situation, the father was abusive and thought to have been part of one of the drug cartels. Pilar was an outgoing, charming little girl . Everyone who came in to the casa hogar fell in love with her. Her brother, Victor, was so shy he could easily disappear into the background. Both were starting to heal from the traumas of their early life.

Pilar and her brother were sent back to their mother at the ages of 10 and 12, respectively. The mother was now "stable." She had a place to live and was in a *pareja* (couple), living with a man who was helping to support her. What the report didn't take into consideration was that the man she was living with and who was supporting her was a *sicario* (a hired killer). As is typical in this lifestyle, the relationship didn't last long.

The year Pilar turned 13, her mother decided to leave her *pareja* with the *sicario* and, in a very desperate move, went to live with a different man —another *sicario*. The greatest horror of all this was for Pilar and Victor.

Victor had entered into the drug business at the age of 13. It would be difficult to even try to imagine what Pilar had experienced in those three years. You don't leave one *sicario* for another *sicario* without consequences. Out of resentment and revenge, Pilar, at the age of 13, was murdered by *sicario* number one. The police took Victor into protective custody. Once in the world of drugs and cartels, it is impossible to escape that world, except, as many say, feet first—dead.

The question of security for our children both inside and outside the casa hogar is very real. The walls around the casa hogar were the same height as around the rehab center behind us where the *ladron* was able to climb over, so after the shootout behind the casa hogar, we raised all the walls another three and a half feet to prevent any unwelcome visitors from being able to stand in the back of a pick up and jump over. After 8 young men were able to come in to the casa hogar at 3 A.M. this past year, we hired a security guard. Criminals all have weapons, but security guards can't carry weapons, and I don't know what they could do if someone tried to violently force their way in. But we hope the uniformed presence would help deter a break-in.

Sometimes we get into situations that are quite dangerous because we are the only option for children caught in violence in our area. DIF (the government social agency) from Michoacan along with the state police had brought three beautiful little children in to the casa hogar for us to care for while the police were "resolving" an issue with the family. I had noticed that these children were not the typical bedraggled, undernourished, disheveled children who are brought in to the casa hogar. They seemed well cared for, clean and well mannered. I looked at their profile. Their grandfather had been murdered in front of them, their mother had to be put in a psychiatric hospital for shock, and then I noticed something else—their last names. Their last names were the names of a very famous drug cartel based in Michoacan. Then I knew the story.

It wasn't long before a man came to the casa hogar to warn us. He was a member of the family and he warned our social worker that we were in a very dangerous situation. Dangerous for all the children at the casa hogar, because if he could find these children, so could the people who wanted them dead, and they wouldn't care who was around. We had better send them somewhere far away because there were people who wanted to see them destroyed along with the rest of their family.

Our social worker called the state authorities and told them the situation, asking them to make arrangements to transfer these poor little children somewhere safe and to remove the danger facing our staff and children would be if they didn't. We don't know where they went or what happened to them, and for security purposes we don't want to know, but I am sure that they will never be able to have a normal life, if a life at all.

Emigdia

Several months ago, police came to the casa hogar to investigate a death. They had a morgue photo of a young woman who had been found dead. She had been murdered fifteen days before, then dumped in a ditch without identification. The police couldn't notify the family until they could positively identify her. The photo was a terrifying photo of a murdered young woman. Because we work with so many children, the police felt there was a possibility that we might have an idea of who she was. Did we know her?

Yes—sad to say, we did.

Emigdia had been brought to us by an aunt as a preteen. She was very emotionally and sexually vulnerable with a syndrome that affected her nervous system and caused her to have high anxiety which also affected her acting out sexually. The psychologist at the hospital put her on medication to help calm her hyperemotional stimulation, and we enrolled her in school. It was difficult for her to concentrate, but little by little, she advanced through junior high school. At 18 years of age, but probably closer to 12 or 13 years of age emotionally, Emigdia went back to live with a family member. Very quickly she became involved with a man who was involved in a prostitution and drug ring. She became pregnant, and as soon as she had her baby, the baby was taken away from her and she was forced into prostitution. Access to her baby was the manipulative power they used over her. She was fighting to get her baby back and planning to run away when she was murdered and her body dumped into a ditch like a bag of trash.

There are too many stories like this. I usually don't openly talk about these, for a variety of reasons....one being safety and personal privacy of the children and the casa hogar, as well as for myself personally. But perhaps it is time for the public to know that what we do is extremely important. We not only rescue these children and change their lives, but also because of the kind of program and vision we have, these children are provided the opportunity to grow and thrive in a safe environment.

When we visited Anabel and her grandmother in a poor area of La Cruz I was reminded how many families live in these conditions. The "house" that Anabel lived in with her grandmother was more like a temporary shelter, a house without walls and a very weak laminate roof that didn't prevent all the rains from coming in. During the rainy season the water would rush down the hill bringing mud and debris into the house. Everything had to be put up high to prevent them from floating down the hill.

Anabel has told a little bit of her story, sharing a very small part of what she has had to go through. I have included Anabel in this section following a few stories that involve cartel activity because Anabel had experiences that brought her into contact with the cartels, prostitution, and the drug world.

There are things that happened to her during the years she was out of the casa hogar that she does not want to share. Some partly because it is too painful, and some because it would be very dangerous for her to share. Anabel has been a blessing for us, and we are excited to see her successfully studying to be a professional chef. Her hope is to be able to do her internship in Spain and then to open her own restaurant. She has had to work hard to put things behind her and to accomplish her goals, but she is determined and it will happen.

Anabel

My name is Anabel, I was born January 17, 1993, and lived with my grandmother Julia and her son from the time I was born. For me, she was my mother. My grandmother did not know how to read or write. She worked in the fields, and I started working in the fields when I was 3 years old. It was my first job. When I entered kindergarten, my grandmother would leave me at 4:00 A.M. close to the kindergarten, because I could not stay in the house since we lived on a hill and it was the only house in the area. We did not have electricity or water. My grandmother's son wanted to abuse me, and that was one of the reasons why I could not stay in the house.

Sometimes I got to stay with the neighbors to wait for my grandmother until she left work. One time it occurred to me to go to the house, and when I saw that my uncle was not there, I decided to stay and clean my grandmother's house. She always arrived tired from work and had to do chores and wash clothes. I wanted to help her.

My grandmother raised me and was like both mother and father. She had so many difficulties and a life full of hard work, but she dedicated herself completely to be with my brothers and me.

My Mamita (my little grandmother) gave us her years, time that she could have used to travel the world or rest, but no, her heart was so big that she preferred to stay and help us move forward.

She was a woman full of love for us, she instilled values—and above all to love others. I have a deep admiration for her—she was a warrior.

She was the best grandmother in the world. She was my energy.

I entered CHLA because we were very poor and had family problems.

Actually, I did not know that the home existed. It was thanks to the president of our colony that my grandmother and I met with Ninfa [a CHLA social worker] about my case, and she was interested in helping my situation.

When I arrived at the casa hogar, it was as if I had arrived in paradise. There were so many happy children playing. For the first time I had drinking water and electric lights and did not have to go to the stream to bathe and wash my clothes or bring water to drink. For the first time I could enjoy a shower and take water from a jug. For the first time I could sleep peacefully without having to be careful not to be bitten by an animal or worry about someone abusing me at night.

For me, Nancy is like a mom I never really had. Being inside the casa hogar completely changed my life and made me see life in another way.

I felt protected and loved and I give thanks for what I am now. I have had the opportunity to travel to places I never imagined.

I always wanted to have a father and when I arrived at the casa hogar I had the opportunity to have a father (Guiber Núñez). I admire him for the love he has given to the children of the casa hogar. He is an example to follow and because of him I know now what it is like to have a father.

Over the years, as I became a little older, I was beginning to notice that my grandmother, who had always been a fighter and strong, became weaker, and I began to worry why none of her children or my brothers supported her. She was the only person who was there for me and so in a certain way, I was her favorite granddaughter and I wanted to be by her side. I felt I needed to do what was my duty. Somehow I had to repay everything she had done for me.

I felt alone with the biggest responsibility in my life. I did not know if I should stay in the casa hogar or be next to my grandmother. I felt between a rock and the wall. My helplessness was so great to see her left alone and none of her children helping her, but I couldn't do anything while I was living inside the casa hogar. I felt frustrated, I cried and then I wiped my tears. At night I thought over and over again what decision should I make to make it the correct one.

It broke my soul to leave the casa hogar, but I decided to be with my grandmother so I could help my family.

After a few years, my Mamita died, and after all I've lived through I felt that again life decided to hit me in the most cruel way, ripping out my heart. I have to struggle with the pain of not seeing Mamita again. It's so difficult, but I'm working on it.

When my grandmother died, I felt completely alone in this world. For me there was no point in continuing living and fighting against life—it did not make sense to me at all. My grandmother was the person I wanted to have by my side, but before she died she made me promise to continue with my studies and look for Nancy. I knew I would be left alone and I knew that for me, Nancy would be like the mom I never had.

From the first day I met her she was like my guardian angel, and although I am not her blood family, she protects me and loves me. Above all I am thankful for my educational opportunities. I am about to finish my undergraduate studies at the university in gastronomy. I am so grateful for the casa hogar, and to God for having put me on the path to my new home.

The casa hogar has given me new life and has taught me to fight for what I want.

Their Mouths Will Be Full! (They Will Have To Eat Their Words!)

We are encouraged to keep working when we see successes. One of those success stories involves two very special brothers, Andrés and Artemio. Many of you who have had the opportunity to visit CHLA know both brothers.

Andrés and Artemio came to us as young boys, barely seven and eight years old, confused and feeling abandoned. They have gone through so many emotional struggles, but their lives took a positive turn when they entered the Casa Hogar Los Angelitos. Both, now young men with college degrees, embarking on successful careers. I asked Andrés how he felt about me putting their story in this book, because when they were going through their teen years, they were very hesitant for people to know their story. Even though others always want to know about the children at the casa hogar, out of respect for their dignity and not wanting to promote a "victim" mentality, we don't talk about the details of their background. However, Andrés as a successful young man said, "I would like to tell my story, because I would like to be an inspiration to others and tell them that they can change their circumstances and their lives if they are determined to do so."

Here is Andrés's story, in his words.

Andrés

My name is Andrés Birrueta Torres. When I was slightly older than one year old, my father was arrested and given a 19-year prison sentence. I lived with my mom, who took care of my baby brother Artemio and me by herself for the next 7 years. I met my dad for the first time in prison when I was 6 years old. I always called him by his formal name, "Mr. Andrés." It was hard to call him "Dad," because for me he was not in my life as a father. I didn't even know who he was. In my mind, I didn't even know why my mom visited the prison. That lasted for two years until I turned 8 years of age. During those two years, my Mom would take us to visit my grandmother in Michoacán and her brother who lived in Cuidád Guzmán. When I was 8, my mom decided to take marijuana into the prison. She was caught and immediately put in prison, sentenced for 8 years. For me and my brother, it was a very hard blow. We were just children who didn't understand what was happening. We only saw that our mother left one day and didn't return. It was when we realized that our mother had not returned that our souls felt like they had been broken into pieces.

The days passed and she still didn't return. Our older sister took care of us for awhile, then one day my father's sister came. We didn't know who she was, but she told us that she was our aunt and that our mother had gone to prison—also that my brother and I would live with her because those were our father's instructions.

We lived approximately 6 months with our father's sister, but we still didn't understand what was happening. There were so many changes in so little time. One day my aunt told us to change clothes and get ready because we were going to leave. We obeyed and we changed. She never mentioned where we would go. What we didn't know was that my aunt had already told my father that it was impossible for her to have us living in her house. Because she had her own children who needed her attention she was going to take us to the government social services—DIF.

When we arrived at the offices of DIF, my aunt went to talk to the social worker. I remember that day and we arrived late at my aunt's house where we had been staying. On the way home she didn't say anything. She didn't tell us what she had talked to the social worker about. She was quiet, and so we were quiet. We got to the house and she gave us dinner and told us that we needed to take a bath so that we could go to sleep.

As small children we didn't really understand what was happening, the only thing we saw and thought was that our parents didn't want us, and because of that we had been left with my aunt.

The next day we got up and my aunt told us to get ourselves dressed and ready. Without knowing what was going to happen we obeyed. In the middle of the day a van came to my aunt's house and we all got in it and left. Our aunt went with us, but we didn't know where we were going or for what reason. I felt lost. That day we got to the casa hogar without knowing where we had been taken.

When we got to this house, the first person I saw was Lupita Carbajal welcoming us and lots of children playing happily. I still didn't know what was happening. I just knew that this was a strange and unknown place. My aunt told us to go play with the other children. and that everything would be fine. As children of 7 and 8 we thought we were only visiting and that we had been taken to know *this place. At that time it didn't pass through my mind that this would be our new home.*

We were playing with the children and when we got bored playing we went to the place where my aunt had been, but she was no longer there. At that moment I felt that the world fell in to me. It was so much, the pain that I felt, because I thought my mother and now my aunt had both abandoned us in that weird and unfamiliar place. That's the first thing a child of 8 thinks. I am alone, lost, Abandoned. During the first days I was always crying because I only wanted to see my mom. My brother Artemio didn't know what was happening and looked to me for his security.

Time passed and we were finally getting used to being in the casa hogar. They enrolled us in a primary school in Santiago where the teachers treated us bad, as if we shouldn't be there. When we would arrive at school, the other kids and some of the teachers always said, "The donkeys of the casa hogar have arrived." When they called us that, we felt embarrassed and we didn't want to keep going to school.

Nancy, who is the founder of Casa Hogar Los Angelitos, was angry and determined to make sure that no one would call us "the donkeys from the casa hogar" anymore and decided to buy a house in Salagua, change schools and bring teachers to help us at the house. All the comments and treatment that damaged us as children changed in the new school. At this new school teachers seemed to want us there and the other children accepted us regardless of where we were from.

I remember in the first year my grade average was 9.4. I was in the top 6 places in the classroom and so I was chosen to participate in some activities, to be the honors escort for the flag. That school ended at the sixth grade. Afterwards I entered the 7th grade at Pablo Lapati. I studied 3 years in that secondary school. During that time I studied, played soccer, entered Ballet folkloric dance, and felt a total transformation in my life. My life was starting to feel normal.

Five years later my mom was released from prison and came to the casa hogar with the husband of my aunt. She was determined to take us out of the casa hogar. She wanted my brother and me with her because we were the youngest of her children. I talked to my brother and told him that we did not want to leave the casa hogar. I said, "Why? Here we are well, we want to study, to make something of ourselves." I made reference to my other brothers, and we did not want to be like them, to work all day in the hot sun—and for that, we needed to study. He told me if that is my decision it was okay with him.

Then my brother and I entered high school to continue our studies.

One day as I was close to graduating from high school, I was talking to Nancy (who I now consider as my mother for everything that she has done for me). I was showing her my grade average, and she congratulated me and told me she was very proud of me, so I said, "Do you remember all those people who called us "the donkeys from the casa hogar"? I answered myself and said, "Well, all of them will have their mouths full, because they can eat their words—I am doing things very well, and I have very good grades."

When I graduated from high school, I went to the United States on a tour to Denver, Colorado, with the folkloric ballet group of the casa hogar. We went to a meeting with a Rotary Club, and there I met Mr. Andrés Osuna. He talked with me and gave me some thoughtful advice— advice that I needed at that moment to make my determination to continue studying. He said, "Opportunity is like a train. Imagine that you are in the train station and you see the train coming. You know that the train is not going to stop for you to get up. It will just slow down so you can get on, and once you are on the train you need to hold on very tight because if you let go you can fall." He said, "Likewise that happens with opportunity. Opportunity is like a train. You see it pass in front of you, you know that it is not going to stop, and you must grab it when it is in front of you and not let go. Like the train, you will regret the opportunity that you missed, what you did not do and you could have done," he told me, "You need to study."

I was motivated by the words of Andrés, so returning to Mexico I did the paperwork to study at the University of Colima, the most prestigious university in the state of Colima. Many aspire to enter that university but not all can enter. I was accepted, and it was the best way to take advantage of all that the casa hogar was doing for me. After 4 years of study, I did my thesis, exam, and all the paperwork to receive my degree.

I always kept in mind the things that Nancy and David, through Casa Hogar Los Angelitos, did for me. I love them as my parents, because they guided me and motivated me, and whenever I failed them they didn't care. They were with me. They listened to me and gave me advice. I finished my degree in International Business.

I thank God for bringing me to the casa hogar and for putting angels in my path—Nancy and David Nystrom. And I want to say thank you to all who supported me and believed in me. Thanks to you, I am now a productive, exemplary person, with principles, values and integrity.

Artemio and Andrés at Andrés' graduation from the University of Colima.

I am so proud of Andrés and his brother Artemio, not only because of the way they have turned their lives around and taken charge of their own futures, but also because of the way they have reframed the narrative of their story. I know so many people in their fifties, sixties, and older who still hold on to angry narratives that they framed in childhood. They insist on holding on to real and perceived hurts that continue to affect their behavior and color perception throughout their lives.

Many times, the potential of people's lives has been stunted, and they get stuck because they embrace what we refer to as a "victim" mentality. It would have been very easy for Andrés and Artemio to do that. But, like Brenda and others who have now continued forward with their education and lives, they didn't give in. I know so many people who are in their fifties, sixties, and even their seventies who still hold on to the angry narrative that they framed in childhood. Holding on to both real and perceived hurts continues to affect their behavior and color perceptions throughout their lives.

When their mother wanted the boys to leave the casa hogar and live with her, Andrés made the difficult emotional decision for himself and his brother Artemio to stay. When he made that decision, he said, "My mother made *her* decision when she decided to take marijuana into the prison. Now *I* am making *my* decision."

You'd think that as intelligent people, we would outgrow those childhood narratives and try to begin to look at things with more balanced attitudes. However, in many situations, our emotions tend to overpower our logic and without a conscious effort to reframe our past and try to understand all the stories that affected us, we just expand and even begin to distort our own narrative to match our perceived hurt. We hold on to the negative rather than trying to heal the hurt by replacing negative emotions with empathy—we don't have to like or deny the actions of others, but perhaps we might try to understand where those actions came from—the time they were in and the emotional circumstances involved. Then we can let ourselves mature into a person who can break that negative cycle. If you live long enough and know enough people, you soon learn that most people went through what they feel is a difficult time in their childhood and early teen years. Those who can look with understanding and empathy at others and forgive can mature into healthier, happier, and personally more successful people. Blackness of thought just creates more blackness.

Transforming Lives

Our innate human desire to create and to express has existed since the beginning of time. As archaeologists have discovered through cave art from thousands of years ago, those who participate in and create art can leave a legacy that lives far beyond their brief years on Earth.

The Expressive Arts program has become an important part of the healing and educational process for the children of the casa hogar and now includes youth from the surrounding community as well.

We began the program in 2005 with folkloric dance classes. Andrés refers to this program in his story, and both he and his brother were very active in the program, as was Brenda. We began incorporating the arts after seeing the difference that involvement in this type of activity made in children's emotional responses. I watched angry, unfocused, volatile children with low self-esteem turn into responsive, self-confident, and educationally successful children.

We found that this program, which included music, folkloric dance, art, language skills, etc., was successful in developing self-discipline, self-confidence, dignity, and physical, mental, and emotional health, which helped to build character and leadership. One of the benefits that comes from the cultural part of the expressive arts is the pride that the children feel for their own culture. They are proud of who they are and where they have come from.

People ask where we got the idea or inspiration to use the arts so extensively in the care and development of the children. It is difficult to say any one thing. I do believe it is a combination of many things: experience, observation, conversation, and inspiration. I was immersed in the arts from an early age, and I know how profoundly I was affected by that experience.

Although I was raised in a humble family, I had the opportunity to study piano for more than twelve years. I also love to sing, and I would sing in small groups and choirs, and I sang solos in my church. I also played a school instrument in the junior high and high school bands and participated in theater from the time I was thirteen years old. I participated in anything I could that didn't require my family to pay extra expense.

I would find private places where I could go and write my heart out, my frustrations, my sadness, my hopes, dreams and angers on scraps of paper or in notebooks. Now, in looking back and thinking about the positive effect of the expressive arts programs for the children of the Casa Hogar Los Angelitos, I believe these activities and the positive mentoring of teachers are directly related to the development of self-confidence, determination and perseverance...the strength of character to never give up regardless of the obstacles.

I believe to be an emotionally healthy person it is important to feel good about who you are, who you have become and where you have come from. My grandfather's family were "share croppers," my great-grandmother became a prostitute in downtown Houston, but to survive they had to be tough. My father was the product of a man who raped a 12-year-old girl, and the family tried to cover that story and so on, but I see now how my family evolved, and I am grateful for the strengths and lives that they passed down to me. We share the DNA of all those who came before us, and, we have the choice to take the combination of all those ancestors, their failures and successes, to become the best we can. But if we are ashamed of who we are and where we come from—if we have not learned empathy and understanding—it affects the way we think about ourselves and every experience in our life. The Mexican people come from a rich heritage of culture, accomplishment, and what were once great empires. However, in today's world, many Mexicans don't recognize the brilliance of their heritage and spend their lives underestimating their own potential. Our ballet folkloric program provides a healthy and exciting way to rediscover an area of that fantastic history and culture.

After watching how our children responded to a pre-hispanic dance performance by the University of Colima, we made the decision to try to incorporate something like that into our activities.

We worked out an agreement with UBAM (a satellite program of the University of Colima) to give our children classes at a discounted cost. However, while we did receive a discount on cost, we still had to pay some, transport the children, and work around everyone's schedules, which limited the number of children who could participate. It was difficult to keep the program working. In 2007, we were able to bring in a teacher, Juan Cruz Martinez, who was teaching at the university.

Juan had been raised by a single mother and didn't know who his father was. When his mother died before Juan turned 10, he lived on the street. He continued going to school and signing his mother's name to papers in order to prevent being picked up by the police. He did this until a neighbor in the area where he was sleeping discovered how extremely sick he was and took him to a hospital. He was diagnosed with severe infestation of his intestines with *lombrices intestinales* and *amebas* (intestinal worms and amoebas). The doctors felt they had no other choice except to remove most of his intestines.

He suffered tremendously, and the people who had taken him to the hospital eventually took him to a casa hogar in Cuernavaca, *Nuestros Pequeños Hermanos*.

Because of his past, Juan had a special place in his heart for the children of CHLA, and he offered to teach as a volunteer at our facilities. He started incorporating all of the children in the classes, and that was the beginning of a new era for Casa Hogar Los Angelitos.

In my first book "*Each Day a Portion*," I talk about Dr. Guiber Nuñez, and the important role that he has played during the early years of the casa hogar. He is now the on-site general director at Casa Hogar Los Angelitos. I have asked Guiber to share in his own words some of his story and the path God has led him on to bring him to this place in life.

> Instruye al niño en su camino, y aun cuando fuere viejo no se apartará de él.
>
> (Train up a child in the way he should go, and when he is old, he will not depart from it.)
>
> —Poverbios 22:6

Dr. Guiber Nuñez Matildes

Casa Hogar los Angelitos has provided a great opportunity to fulfill what I believe God has placed in my life to be my mission. I have wondered many times why I was put in contact with Casa Hogar Los Angelitos, but now I believe I know.

When my maternal grandmother (Elisa Ramírez García) was on her deathbed, she told my mother and my sister that she had a vision or a message from God.

"I am not angry with God that my son Guiber is far from here. He is in Manzanillo, fulfilling a mission that God has given him. Some men dressed in white visited me this morning, and they explained the reason why Guiber must be in Manzanillo and not here with me."

I firmly believe that the casa hogar project is a project of God, and things that have happened are in the time and will of God.

There are two events I relate to my grandmother's comment. The first event happened when I was about 9 or 10 years old, while in the cane fields eating with my grandfather. I tried to open a soft drink with my machete, but instead the lid of the bottle flew into my eye. There was a lot of blood and I knew I had a serious problem because I only saw white and was in a lot of pain. I remember my grandfather checked me, prayed for me, and told me to return home because he had to continue working.

On the way home I was so afraid I would be blind.

I thought about how I heard how God wanted the sacrifice to be pure and I was thinking it must be important to be complete, and that must include sight. So in my 9 year-old mind I decided to make a deal with God. I closed my eyes and asked God to heal me, I said, "God when I grow up I want to be a preacher, to talk to people about you, and I know that you do not want a one-eyed preacher, please help me and heal my eye.

By night time the doctor had come and gave me medication and put a patch on my eye. I again asked God to heal me.

Even today I remember my prayer: "God, I know that if a person has faith the size of a mustard seed, they can tell the mountains to move, and they will move; so on this nigh, I'm asking you to move that little mountain that is in front of my house, and...I'm asking you to heal my eye." The next day when I woke up the first thing I did was to see if the mountain had moved, I was sad to see that it was still there, however I had asked for two things, and it was necessary to verify whether or not my eye was healing.

So I carefully removed the patch from my eye and I was able to see the silhouette of a fan that was above my bed. I put the patch on again and thanked God because I knew he was healing my eye.

I felt committed to God since I had asked for a personal favor that he would heal me.

I believe HE did heal me.

The second event connected to the words of my grandmother happened In April 1999. After a Christian event in our community we were all going to a beach in the state of Guerrero. Our destination was Playa "Ventura" and the goal was to have a family day on the beach.

When passing through a town called "La Union," a vehicle similar to those used by the police filled with men dressed in blue police uniforms started following us. They followed us until we reached a deserted place on the highway and then they began shooting at us, wounding two of my cousins and me. I was hit by a bullet in the abdomen and another in the thigh.

Moments of my life passed through my mind. When I looked at the bullet hole in my abdomen *and began to taste blood in my mouth, I knew that my life was in danger. But I thought if I have to die, this is a good day for dying.*

I was sure that if I did die I would be with God. But then the memory of my commitment to God to preach his word sounded in my head. Something told me that I would not die despite having two bullets in my body, it was clear to me that I still had to preach His word. I did not know where or when, but I was sure that God had plans for my life. The armed vehicle turned around and finally we found a military post with a medic further down the road. They began to help those who had been shot.

I had just graduated from medical school and I knew that the bullets in my body could not be safely taken out. The main thing was to stop the bleeding. No surgery was performed on me, and for the second time I understood that the one in control of my life was God. I knew that he had literally saved me from death and that I still had a commitment to fulfill.

I didn't know anything about Casa Hogar Los Angelitos or where I would possibly fulfill this commitment with GOD. However, it was clear that I still had to preach His word.

For me, studying medicine was a great challenge. My mother, Hermelinda Matildes Ramírez, was supportive of my career in every way possible, but with a tremendous amount of effort and sacrifice. She motivated me with phrases like "You have to finish your medical career," "Determine yourself," and " I want to see you one day sitting behind a desk treating patients."

I was living in Acapulco, going to school, studying, without resources, and many times I thought about giving up. However, thinking about the field work, planting corn, Jamaica, rice, beans, all the hard work that a farmer has to plant and harvest his products and then to sell them at a very low price, and the words of my mom saying, "My dream is to see you as a doctor," I knew I had to keep working to make it happen. I had the motivation to continue.

Studying was a big challenge, and finishing my career was a great achievement. Only a very small percentage of the population of my state complete high school and even fewer continue to study a career.

When I finished medical school, I came to serve my undergraduate internship in Manzanillo, Colima, where

Preparing for a fiesta.

I met my wife, Emily Carbajal López. She is originally from Manzanillo, Colima, and I met her when I was working in the civil hospital of Manzanillo. She was a nurse. A beautiful nurse.

We were married in 2000, and for a few months we lived in Tecoanapa, in the state of Guerrero, working as a doctor and nurse in a very poor mountain community called El Charco. That community was my inspiration for the program "Ministries of Love," which I presented to Nancy

Little Angel practicing guitar.

Folkloric Dance brings beauty and self-confidence into the lives of children.

Nystrom years later and which was implemented at CHLA.

My wife and I found ourselves living in a situation of extreme poverty, without drinking water or adequate food to eat. The people in this little mountain pueblo had chickens, but very little more. So, we had eggs and tortillas for breakfast, tortillas and eggs for lunch and tortillas for dinner. The young people had the desire to study but with very few possibilities.

The priority was to till the land, plant the fields for self-consumption, and simply try to have food to eat. Although I was a medical doctor, we began to teach reading and writing, since many people there could not read or write. However, our contract was terminated because we were doing too many things to help the people and that was not part of our contract. We were not given contracts, so we decided to return to Manzanillo.

In Manzanillo, it was difficult to get a job; however, it was not as difficult as in Guerrero.

In 2001, I met Nancy Nystrom through my sister-in-law, Lupita Carbajal. And I was introduced to Casa Hogar Los Angelitos. I soon became interested in the project. Nancy and Lupita invited me to be part of the casa hogar program, but at that time I was saturated with work in Manzanillo, just trying to make a living. I was working at the hospital in Cihuatlan, Jalisco, and the Civil Hospital of Manzanillo covering emergencies and accidents. I didn't think it was a good offer to work with the casa hogar because it had already taken a lot of effort and time to find the jobs I had.

However, after seriously praying about the offer, I decided to install my private office in Casa Hogar Cyber Café, located a few blocks from the main casa hogar facilities. We took our savings and remodeled an area to have a medical care space. Three months after starting with the office the landlord gave notice to vacate that space. This was really bad news for me. I was very frustrated because I had invested my savings in furniture and equipment and an office that I now had to remove.

Nancy and Lupita talked to me and offered me a space inside *the facilities of the casa hogar. I was not excited about another move, and especially to a location that didn't have any traffic, but again I went to God seeking guidance on this new decision. As I was reading the Bible, I found a scripture that said*

> But seek first the kingdom of God and his righteousness, and all these things will be added to you.
>
> —Mat. 6:33

This verse gave me my answer, so even though I didn't know how it could work for me, I agreed to bring my practice inside the casa hogar. Now we had a place to take my office furniture and an office. Nancy and I agreed that I would work in my office on weekends and the rest of the days I would work to help the children of Casa Hogar Los Angelitos.

The first weekend that I arrived at the casa hogar to start my consultation, I was surprised to see a number of cars parked outside the facility. My reaction again was frustration with this situation, thinking, "The first day of my consultation—my first weekend of work inside the casa hogar—and Nancy is having a party?! That's not fair!"

But as I entered the gate a person at the door asked "Are you the doctor?" and then I saw there were more people sitting on the benches outside my new office waiting for me.

In the past, I probably had no more than three or four patients per day. That first weekend I attended to approximately 30 people! God opened the windows of heaven and blessed me, and that began my long collaborative relationship with Casa Hogar Los Angelitos.

For many years, I was in charge of various programs. One of them, Ministerios de Amor, *we began in 2001. The objective was to help people in desperate or vulnerable situations, especially in my home state of Guerrero. During those 8 years I supported the operation area as well as the administrative area.*

However, After 8 years I was again becoming frustrated because of the emotional connections I developed with the children, seeing them grow and develop and then seeing them removed without their consent. The families wanted to take them as they became old enough to help support the family. It was difficult for me to watch dreams and futures destroyed when they left Casa Hogar Los Angelitos. Girls who, shortly after leaving the casa hogar, became pregnant or children who started using or selling drugs. This frustration began to affect my emotional aspect.

I understand now that I did not have the necessary emotional tools to deal with these situations. I also felt that something was missing in the casa hogar. I felt that each child needed better tools to face life.

Life in Mexico is very complicated. Pursuing a career seems to be tailored to those who already have more. For people with low economic resources it is very difficult. Entering a university is almost exclusively for people who have high economic resources. For the peasants and the poor, it is complicated if not impossible. There is a mentality in Mexico that if you do not have monetary resources you will never achieve them. It is a poverty mentality...a mentality of defeat that many people have. As a people, a culture, we have been made to believe that if you do not already have, *you can never* have. *It is your fate in life.*

This situation really affected me because I realized that it was necessary to change this mentality in myself first before I could change it in others.

When I left the casa hogar, I was frustrated, feeling incomplete and angry. My intention from the day that I left the casa hogar was to work on myself and prepare myself for some day, in God's time, to return with better tools, new forces, and new programs. I stopped being at the casa hogar in the operational area, but even from the outside, I dreamed of returning and contributing new things so that the children who entered had better opportunities to learn, grow, develop, and heal.

My wife who was continuing her studies for a degree in Psychology and a Masters in Gestalt Therapy invited me to a workshop called "Rescuing Your Inner Child." This workshop helped me to realize the problems and conflicts from my own childhood. Problems that I had not resolved with my father, mainly the issue of abandonment. He separated from my mom when I was a small child. Living without a father at school festivals where children ask "Why is it that your dad won't come to see you dance? ...your dad won't come to see you say a poem? Or...see you in a parade?" Those moments filled my head with

Emily and Dr. Guiber.

resentment, when I realized that **I** was a child abandoned by my father. In reality, my mom was also absent, although at that age I could justify it in my reasoning because she went to work away from home to earn money and give us an education, to see her leave in the truck after Some days with us was terrible. I remember that when my mom boarded the bus to go to Huamuxtitlan, Guerrero (where she worked as a nurse in a hospital), my sister and I ran behind crying. Those were painful moments.

Through this workshop, "Rescuing Your Inner Child," I realized the importance of honoring my parents through forgiving them, one of the biblical principles is to honor your parents, so I started a personal therapeutic journey. Later, at the suggestion of my wife, I started a Masters in Gestalt Therapy, which served to provide me with important tools to heal unresolved situations in my own life. In addition, this education allowed me to start with the development of programs I designed and to work with the children of Casa Hogar Los Angelitos In collaboration with my wife.

After 8 long years away from the operational aspect of the casa hogar, Nancy, through Lupita Carbajal, approached my wife and me to create

Just hanging out.

a program to support the children and adolescents who live in Casa Hogar los Angelitos. So this proposal was a call again from God, and we started the programs that we had already prepared.

In addition, we initiated a spiritual program on Sundays at 5:00 P.M. where biblical subjects are taught without using doctrines other than the Bible and teaching the love of God. We became involved in the general operation and administration of the casa hogar once again. But this time I was prepared and ready.

In every child and adolescent who lives at the casa hogar, I see people with changed lives. The support of each sponsor, each company, and each institution that brings resources to the casa hogar is a great blessing for these children and young people. The dedication and lives of Nancy and David Nystrom give new hope.

Currently, Casa Hogar Los Angelitos has great programs that I now direct, continually praying for God's understanding and wisdom.

My goal is to be sure that each child upon arrival at this Home is received by all the staff... to welcome him, to make him feel wanted, to offer support, love, and our attention through educated, capable housemothers who can give good care—to be sure they receive psychotherapy attention in order to work through their unresolved conflicts. In addition to therapeutic workshop programs within the casa hogar, therapy is provided outside the casa hogar through summer camps, field trips, and programs such as scouting and interaction with the community.

It is vital that each child has attention to their integral physical health—also that they have support for school tasks and, in addition to reinforcing educational learning, that they have development opportunities through music, dance, English, and other expressive arts classes. It is our goal to motivate each child to follow their dreams, to teach them that with effort and courage, anything can be achieved.

Casa Hogar Los Angelitos has been a great opportunity for me to fulfill God's plan for my life, to preach His word, to instruct and to teach the great special love that God has for each and every child.

> *I am blessed to know Nancy and David, and I thank God that he has put so many great people in my life, including my grandfather, Nicolás Matildes Zúñiga, who, along with my grandmother, taught me the way to live a life of integrity and principles; my mother, for teaching me not to give up and who showed me that if you want something bad enough you can do it; my wife Emily and my daughters Yareli and Nicole who accompany me in this project Casa Hogar Los Angelitos.*

TOTAL BLESSINGS!

The Continuation

It seems like only yesterday that Casa Hogar Los Angelitos existed only in that small storefront on a back corner street in Salagua, feeding 100–125 children one hot meal per day. That was in November 1995. Then in June of 1996 opening the doors of a full-time care facility in downtown Santiago. It seems only yesterday … and yet at the same time it seems like such a long time ago. So many bridges to cross, and mountains to climb! Thousands of children's lives, both through the casa hogar and within the community have been affected. Young people and adults from other areas who have taken the time to visit and to actually "see" the hearts of the children, have had their lives changed as a result.

"It is easier to build strong children than repair broken men."
—*Frederick Douglas*

Healing Journey program.

When I began this work, I was told, "It won't last." People didn't want to invest in something that was destined to fail. Twenty-two years ago, a local businessman openly voiced that silent (and sometimes not so silent) opinion as I tried to seek help and support in my quest to feed hungry children. "I'm not going to give anything, or get involved…it will never last—she's a woman *and* a foreigner!!"

One politically prominent woman snarled, "I can't *stand* that woman!" when my name was mentioned. No particular reason—just resenting the fact that I existed in "her" world. It soon became clear to me that people who had the power to do the things I was trying to do—but who weren't doing them—would resent someone else coming in (especially a foreigner!) and proving it could be done.

Lupita Carbajal (now Nystrom) and I were under arrest for trying to do things in a different way. People wanted the property we had purchased for the casa hogar, and that was a way to get it. We carried an *ampara* (legal protection) with us to prevent being picked up and thrown in jail. And even two years after Lupita and I were acquitted of any wrongdoing, I was told, "There is still a warrant for your arrest on file."

Above: "Big brother" Andrés mentoring the younger children.

Below: Making the job worthwhile.

Putting It Together

In putting this book together, there were many people who said, "You have presented stories of the children and information regarding the problems...but what are solutions, what can help?"

In earlier pages, I talk a little about the type of care and atmosphere we feel is important in helping our children, including giving them a sense of self-value, acceptance, unconditional love, family, educational opportunity, and a style of discipline that educates instead of punishes. I believe that the most important thing that we can give each child is a foundation of security and the belief that God loves them and that their life has value. Many times, children who enter CHLA come with a sense of abandonment and lack of self-worth. They all suffer emotional traumas from their early history.

How can a child develop and become successful if they are in emotional pain and feel their life has no worth?

It is not always clear or easy to know how to accomplish these goals and no question, there will be mistakes along the way. But we have to try.

Through the years, we have encouraged professionals to bring programs and studies to help us learn how to work better with our children, our workers, and ourselves. We invite such organizations as Kidz@heart (teachers teaching other teachers how to work with children) and specialists working with children suffering from trauma such as professor Dr. Don Phelps at Aurora University in Chicago, and programs such as "Empowered To Connect." We try to incorporate other educational and workshop programs throughout each year that we feel fit the mission and vision of caring for the children of CHLA.

In 2015, we began a program called "Healing Journey" with the intention of providing support for our children, enabling them to have a higher success rate healing from the traumas of their past. This program was established under the leadership of Lic Emily Carbajal Lopez, PSY, ENF Graf, Mtra Terapia Guestalt, and Dr. Guiber Nuñez, M. The following is Emily's story.

Dr. Guiber and some of the children.

Emily Carbajal López

I think that the reason I am at Casa Hogar Los Angelitos is because of everything that I have lived—all the good things as well as the not-so-good Experiences that allowed me to grow and learn, but above all sensitized me to want to give the best of myself.

I come from a humble family made up of my parents and eleven siblings—eight women and three men. I think my childhood was good; however, coming from a big family, I soon realized that educational opportunities for me did not exist. After finishing primary school there was nothing more, so I began to insist daily for the next four years to be given the opportunity to continue studying. When I would insist my father always answered in frustration "I wanted to give my children everything and hoped that they would have the opportunity to study, but daughter, I cannot. How can I make that happen? I do not know how!"

At Casa Hogar Los Angelitos, I see so many children who are hungry to improve themselves just as I was, but they come from dysfunctional families who can't give them what they do not have. They have a hunger like the one I had to overcome. I wanted to study, to be prepared, but for my parents it was almost impossible to give me that opportunity.

After insisting every day for four years one day my father reluctantly said, "Okay, go to school!"

We lived on a ranch in the mountains without much transportation so I had no idea what I might have to do. I had graduated from elementary school, and finally my father decided to send me to live with a family that I found to be very uncomfortable and difficult to be with. That situation only lasted two months before I left to go live at my father's brother's house, which was even more difficult. After discussing the difficulty of the living situations my father sent me to live with a cousin's wife, that didn't go well either. I was frustrated with the abusive situations I was put in and didn't know how I was going to be able to continue. Finally, my father found another family who lived outside Colima, and I was able to live with them for a year in order to finish my high school.

I realized during this time that it is not always your blood family that you should be with. With this family I felt accepted, loved and protected. I finished high school in Colima and then returned to live in Manzanillo. I was now older, and I started to work and knew I wanted to study a professional career. I began to look for this opportunity.

I decided to study nursing and ended up working for the Mexican Navy for three years so that I could get my education there. When I left the Navy I fell in love and married my husband, Dr.Guiber Nuñez.

My sister Lupita Carbajal was administrator for the children's home Casa Hogar Los Angelitos and in 2000, I began as a volunteer there. At that time, I worked as a nurse, and I identified difficulties among the teenagers with interaction (problems with impulsive behaviors during group work or activities). Many of the children felt guilty because they were living in a good environment and living better than their family. Many times, the family tries to take advantage of them. When they see the children growing and becoming successful, they use the manipulation of guilt to pull them out to go to work for the family. When that happens the dreams of doing something more with their life is over. This situation affected me a lot. I wanted to help, and I think I did help but it was not enough.

I studied psychology and I thought...now I could help more, but the help was still not enough. I felt I needed better tools to help empower them I began researching programs that I thought might help the children. In 2008 I made a decision to travel to Guadalajara every week from my home to study for a masters in Gestalt therapy. Receiving my degree in the year 2012.

In 2015, I started my research project: RECOGNITION AND EXPRESSION OF EMOTIONS IN THE ADOLESCENTS OF 14 TO 17 YEARS OF AGE AT CASA HOGAR LOS ANGELITOS THROUGH WORKSHOPS WITH THE GESTALTIC APPROACH. This is where I used the technique of recording written discourse through evaluations at the beginning and final evaluations of the adolescents.

In this research, I found that the recognition and expression of emotions allowed the children to know and express themselves in a more assertive manner. Through these techniques ,they identified and recognized emotions that sensitized them to become more aware of their behavior and allowed them to experience important changes in themselves. The work is not easy, but it is so rewarding when I see each child begin to change and develop a healthy self-perspective. I feel a deep connection with the children and believe that this is where God wants me to be.

My training and life experiences have brought me to a place where I feel I can help the children move forward and heal.

Emily Carbajal

Emily spends much of her time in activities with the children, developing a sense of trust and caring that enables the children to talk and share their hurts and dreams in a natural way.

This past year one of the children, a beautiful and energetic little two-year-old girl, kept saying to Emily "My baby, my baby," looking at Emily as if to say *help me find my baby.* Assuming that the little girl had lost her doll and was looking for it, Emily began to talk with her more about her baby. It was obvious that her baby was very important to her—she missed her baby, and she wanted to find it.

Researching little Lupita's history, Emily discovered that the baby Lupita was looking for was her baby sister. Lupita, at the tender age of two, had witnessed the murders of her mother and her baby sister.

This tragic scene was imprinted so deeply on her delicate little heart and mind that she had been unable to remove it from her thoughts, and she continued to look for "her baby."

Lupita was found by the police on the street wandering alone. Somehow, she had managed to escape the massacre in her home and was walking around, unaware of her surroundings. She was taken to the authorities and then to us.

Since no one knew her name, she named herself. There were two other girls in the casa hogar with the name Lupita. One girl was 17, and one girl was 10. So Lupita decided she wanted to be called *Lupita Chiquita* (little Lupita), and when asked her name, that is what she calls herself. She is an amazing little girl. A miracle of survival.

The traumas that many of our children suffer are heartbreaking and difficult to even imagine.

Three of our children were brought to us because their mother committed suicide (or it was made to look like a suicide). But the hardest part of that was that it was her nine-year-old son who had found his mother hanging in the house. For a long time, it was impossible to get him to talk or interact with the other children. He was so traumatized by the scene that he was unable to remove it from his mind. It took years of working with Luis to finally begin to remove the blackness that surrounded him.

The methods Emily uses helps the children to release the bad and replace it with something different.

I consider it important to mention that working at the casa hogar helps me to connect with my own history and resources, both emotional and cognitive, which then helps me to achieve each of the goals I set for my own self in life.

During my time at Casa Hogar Los Angelitos I have used different techniques, according to the need of each child, because the same thing does not work for everyone, However what I see that has worked for me, has been to treat each child as a desired child, to convey that we really want to have them with us, and that we love them. For me there is a big difference between a desired child and one who is not wanted.

Always making them feel they are not alone, by giving them a space that provides confidence and the security to express themselves. This is important especially in the face of all the social problems that many children and teenagers in the casa hogar have experienced and continue to experience.

All this is done to empower the children to acquire the necessary tools in order to conduct

> *themselves in their lives and address the daily problems they face. The fact of being interned in a home such as Casa Hogar Los Angelitos by their relatives represents abandonment for them.*
>
> *—Emily Carbajal*

Both my husband Dave and I applied for Mexican citizenship so that we could participate in the legal activities necessary on behalf of the casa hogar. When the results came in, I was told, "Your husband has been accepted for citizenship...but you are denied."

In reality, the businessman was correct in his presumption of failure, as I have discovered over the years. A visitor who had been involved in Rotary International projects like ours all over the world was visiting the casa hogar a few years ago, and at the end of the evening he asked the question, "How long have you been doing this?" I said, "This will be 19 years..."

He interrupted. "Well, that says a lot—the very fact that you have lasted that long. Most projects like this are begun by women after a loss of some kind, and 95% don't last more than 5 years." They all began with good intentions, but as many have discovered, good intentions alone don't always carry you through.

I was having coffee with a friend—one of my former TCF board members who was also a personal friend for a number of years. We were talking about some of the difficulties that I had been dealing with (government officials trying to shut us down, being put under arrest—a few other little things like that). I was sharing a few incidents with him, and I have to admit I was surprised and did not expect his response when he asked, "Why do so many people dislike you?!"

Whoa! What??! I sucked in my breath trying to decide if he were serious or being sarcastic or joking. I have never thought of myself as someone that "so many people" would "dislike." As a

Sisters Emily López and Lupita Carbajal Nystrom.

matter of fact, I often overcompensate just so people *will* like me.

I grew up a little shy around people (like many others), so I worked hard at trying to be a friendly, happy, I-love-everybody kind of person. How could someone who knew me *as a friend* ask me, "Why do so many people dislike you?" Why did he think that? How could he even think "so many people" disliked me? I was really hurt!

I answered defensively, "That's not true! Only a few people don't like me—just the ones who don't want to see me succeed!"

One of my favorite Bible stories takes place during the time when Nehemiah was trying to rebuild the wall of Jerusalem after it had been destroyed, remaining in ruins, and easily overrun by those who continued to damage the city. The people of Jerusalem had not taken the initiative or bothered to repair or rebuild. They just left it in ruins. Nehemiah, who had been part of the remnant that had been taken into captivity many years before, felt it was a disgrace to allow the city of his ancestors to remain in ruins. He felt "called" to return, and he gathered dedicated people together to help do the work.

Once the wall had begun, some of the people in the surrounding area began to mock him and make fun of the wall, saying it would never last—"That stone wall would collapse if even a fox walked on top of it!"

Taunts didn't stop the progress, so they began shooting arrows at Nehemiah trying to create confusion and fear.

Nehemiah met with his people and gave instructions: *This is the Lord's work, and He will protect us.* However, he also included some common sense along with his faith: *Carry your shield in one hand and build with the other hand until we have completed this work.* That's what they did, and the wall was finally built.

There are always those who are quick to criticize and look for or manufacture problems rather than lift up and support. I guess it has been part of human nature for thousands of years. However, I am still surprised when people in my own personal sphere look for reasons to disenfranchise or to influence others to give up. I just don't get it. I really question whether we need so many "devil's advocates."

Years ago, a friend reminded me of a popular but cynical expression: "No good deed goes unpunished." So throughout these years, I have learned to try to stay focused, keep my vision, and stand strong with my shield in one hand and a building brick in the other, prepared for those arrows to come.

I am reminded by my friend Kevin Skeens of a fable from the sixth century:

The Man, the Boy, and the Donkey

A man and his son were once going with their donkey to market. They were walking along by its side when a countryman passed them and said, "You fools, what is a donkey for but to ride upon?"

So the man put the boy on the donkey and they went on their way. But soon they passed a group of men, one of whom said, "See that lazy youngster—he lets his father walk while he rides."

So the man ordered his boy to get off and got on himself. But they hadn't gone far when they passed two women, one of whom said to the other, "Shame on that lazy lout to let his poor little son trudge along."

Well, the man didn't know what to do, but at last he took his boy up before him on the donkey. By this time they had come to the town, and the passers-by began to jeer and point at them. The man stopped and asked what they were scoffing at. The men said, "Aren't you ashamed of yourself for overloading that poor donkey of yours—you and your hulking son?"

The man and boy got off and tried to think what to do. They thought and they thought. At last, they cut down a pole, tied the donkey's feet to it, and raised the pole and the donkey to their shoulders, carrying the donkey. They went along amidst the laughter of all who met them till they came to market bridge, when the donkey, getting one of his feet loose, kicked out and caused the boy to drop his end of the

I See You 157

pole. In the struggle, the poor donkey fell over the bridge and, his fore-feet being tied together, he drowned.

"That will teach you," said an old man who had followed them.

> ***"TRY TO PLEASE ALL***
> ***AND YOU WILL PLEASE NONE."***

You can change the characters and the circumstances, but the underlying truth is still obvious.

Where there is no vision, the people perish.
—*Proverbs 29:18*

There are the ongoing questions of *why* and *how*: *Why* is it important to know how to move out of poverty? *How* does that affect a person's ability to achieve goals or function in society? *How* do we develop an atmosphere where children can truly thrive and move out of their poverty mentality and self-defeating behavior?

I can give all kinds of examples and programs that create the right atmosphere; however, I think that Dorothy Law Nolte very aptly sums up the 'how' to help a child develop, grow, and become a successful member of society.

Children Learn What They Live

If children live with criticism, they learn to condemn.
If children live with hostility, they learn to fight.
If children live with fear, they learn to be apprehensive.
If children live with pity, they learn to feel sorry for themselves.
If children live with ridicule, they learn to feel shy.
If children live with jealousy, they learn to feel envy.
If children live with shame, they learn to feel guilty.

If children live with encouragement, they learn confidence.
If children live with tolerance, they learn patience.
If children live with praise, they learn appreciation.
If children live with acceptance, they learn to love.
If children live with approval, they learn to like themselves.
If children live with recognition, they learn it is good to have a goal.

If children live with sharing, they learn generosity.
If children live with honesty, they learn truthfulness.
If children live with fairness, they learn justice.
If children live with kindness and consideration, they learn respect.
If children live with security, they learn to have faith in themselves and in those about them.
If children live with friendliness, they learn the world is a nice place in which to live.

—©1972 by Dorothy Law Nolte

CHLA has gone through many challenges, yet we have stayed focused on maintaining the original vision. Over the years our methods have proven to be successful, and we have become a model that I believe is possible to duplicate throughout the world.

So many lives have changed and been given opportunity for success, as well as educational and economic opportunity and hope for the future.

Appendix

- 1 billion people around the world live in extreme poverty.
- Trillions of dollars have been spent to relieve poverty.

It might be worthwhile to consider that sometimes what we do and the money we spend may have unintended consequences. When our desire to help gets in the way of others being productive, our actions might have a long-term negative effect on the community and be more of a hindrance than a help.

Love demands that we act…but also to act humbly and wisely and pay to attention to the effects of our help. Moving from aid to production requires economic and job development.

To obtain a quality job, you have to have a level of training to match that job and a path to get there with skills, training, and education.

High-quality education must be made available and affordable if people are to be pulled out of poverty. It must have not only a heart but also a mind for the poor by working with the local culture intelligently and with compassion.

Compassion is not pity or a point of view. Compassion is action and seeks independence, human dignity, self-esteem, and self-confidence for those for whom we have compassion.

- 63% of youth suicides are from fatherless homes (*U.S. Dept. Of Health/Census*)—5 times the average.
- 90% of all homeless and runaway children are from fatherless homes—32 times the average.
- 85% of all children who show behavior disorders come from fatherless homes—20 times the average. (*Center for Disease Control*)
- 80% of rapists with anger problems come from fatherless homes –14 times the average. (*Justice & Behavior,* Vol 14, pp. 403–426)
- 71% of all high school dropouts come from fatherless homes—9 times the average.

(National Principals' Association Report)

...but true religion is caring for the widows and fatherless [orphans] in their time of need.

James 1:27

References

The Ballad of "Galloping Hogan"

Old Limerick is in danger
And Ireland is not free;
So Scarsfield sends a message
To a fearless rapparee.
"Come ride across the Shannon
At the sounding of the drum
And we'll blow the enemy siege train
To the land of Kingdom Come.

Chorus

Galloping Hogan, Galloping Hogan,
Galloping all along,
In his saddle is a sabre,
On his lips there is a song;
He's off across the Shannon,
To destroy the enemy cannon;
And he goes galloping, he goes galloping,
Galloping, galloping on…

The rapparee is bearded.
There's a twinkle in his eye:
As he rides into the city,
The Limerick ladies cry:
"Mr. Outlaw Mr. Outlaw,
Will you tarry here with me?"
"Och! I'm off to Ballyneety,
To blow up a battery!"

So tonight along the Shannon,
By the pale light of the moon,

> There flows an eerie brightness,
> As of an Indian noon;
> Then clippody-clop responding
> Through the lattice of the shade
> The ghost of Galloping Hogan
> Goes a-riding down the glade.
>
> —*Traditional*

Our heroes can strongly affect the developing image we have of ourselves.

Throughout the years, volunteers have visited to help with various projects at the casa hogar and in the community. One of the earliest groups were volunteers from LifeSpring, a church in Loveland, Colorado, that has become a continuous support for us, sending groups down each year and helping to complete various projects.

After one of those early trips, Gene Milway, a volunteer from LifeSpring, wrote the following poem.

1. 'Twas down a long way to Santiago Bay
   From Life Spring Covenant Church,
   For a volunteer mission to improve the condition
   Of an orphanage left in the lurch.

   On a dusty dirt street where land and sea meet
   In the bustling seaport of Manzanillo
   Sits a haven for waifs whose life was n'er safe
   It's Casa Hogar, Mexico.

   There were evil minds that were oh so blind
   To the poverty and to the need,
   Yet a vision came forth, from a woman up North
   With the courage to go forward and lead.

Our heroes can strongly affect the developing image we have of ourselves.

    Then blessings did follow, with tough times to swallow
    But still a compound was acquired.
    'Twas an adequate place, enhanced by grace
    And run by a staff inspired.

    This peaceful spot is only a dot
    In the hopeless misery of many
    But by the prayers of compassionate players
    Help comes from a land of plenty.

2. Now there was much to be done in the heat of the sun
    For Casa Hogar upgrade and repair
    So paint brushes splashed and paint rollers slashed
    While a beautician cut everyone's hair.

    Then our mason's chore as in days of yore
    Was mixing the mortar, then trowel,

So the work was hard and all over the yard
Yet we saw nary a frown or scowl

Many piñatas were made, under banana tree shade
And the screens were replaced all around.
Then a computer genius blocked all things heinous
And left their computer quite sound.

A slide and a swing and a jungle gym thing
Was assembled in a record four days,
And a fine mural wall that was painted by all
Left even the artists amazed.

A dentist inspected to see if teeth were neglected
And was happy to report a clean bill.
So the love that we felt simply made our hearts melt
And the memory remains with us still.

3. Now a project completed disguises what's needed
For in spite of the progress we made
Ongoing shortfalls bring additional stalls
To a vision and plans that were laid

To lift up these lil' kids and remove those slick skids
That start them down deadly grim trails.
We must search our own heart, step in and take part
To prove once again that love never fails.

There is joy and good nature in these children for sure
We see it in their studies and play,
We have felt their embrace, see smiles on their face
Yet their eyes long for love every day.

To experience firsthand the poor children of the land
And to see the great promise within.
When the orphanage becomes their mentor and home
Promoting their growth while protecting from sin,

Is reason to be grateful and ever so thankful
For all of the dedicated, deserving souls,
Who spend so unselfishly their energy so gracefully
To point a child toward worthwhile goals.

—Gene Milway 2003

Behold, I send an angel before you to guard you on your way and to bring you to the place I have prepared.

—*Exodus 23:20*

drawing by Gene Milway

Casa Hogar Los Angelitos
(The House of the Little Angels)

1. Angels are messengers of importance
   Bringing instructions from God, who
   In Fatherly love leaves naught to chance.
   In mystical fashion they may appear
   In dreams or various forms to be sure,
   Yet, fear not, their role is divinely clear
   And one must know the Lord is near.

2 Now, earthly angels, no less, also exist
   Appearing magically before our eyes
   Calling us to a service that's hard to resist.
   Where poverty, hunger, abuse, and neglect
   Result in despair for the helpless ones,
   Angels of love step in to correct
   And little children gain self-respect.
   Do you believe in Angels?

   —*Gene and Gaea Milway*

But the Greatest Gift Is Love!

1. Though I speak with the tongues of men and of angels, but have not love, I have become sounding brass or a clanging cymbal.
2. And though I have the gift of prophecy, and understand all mysteries and all knowledge, and though I have all faith, so that I could remove mountains, but have not love, I am nothing.
3. And though I bestow all my goods to feed the poor, and though I give my body to be burned, but have not love, it profits me nothing.
4. Love suffers long and is kind; love does not envy; love does not parade itself, is not puffed

up;
5. does not behave rudely, does not seek its own, is not provoked, thinks no evil;
6. does not rejoice in iniquity, but rejoices in the truth;
7. bears all things, believes all things, hopes all things, endures all things.
8. Love never fails. But whether there are prophecies, they will fail; whether there are tongues, they will cease; whether there is knowledge, it will vanish away.
9. For we know in part and we prophesy in part.
10. But when that which is perfect has come, then that which is in part will be done away.
11. When I was a child, I spoke as a child, I understood as a child, I thought as a child; but when I became a man, I put away childish things.
12. For now we see in a mirror, dimly, but then face to face. Now I know in part, but then I shall know just as I also am known.
13. And now abide faith, hope, love, these three; but the greatest of these is love.

—I Cor. 1–13

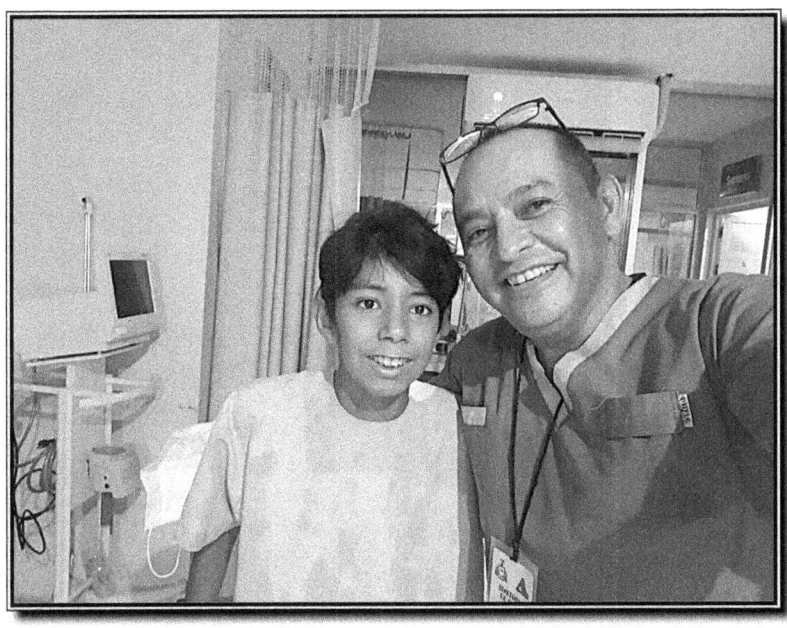

Please consider supporting
Casa Hogar Los Angelitos
with your tax-deductible gift
by going to *tcfcares.org*.

Watch for the special documentary
UNCONDITIONAL
Presenting the story of
CASA HOGAR LOS ANGELITOS

www.ingramcontent.com/pod-product-compliance
Lightning Source LLC
Chambersburg PA
CBHW061645040426
42446CB00010B/1585